ODD LOTS

ODD LOTS

Seasonal Notes of a City Gardener

Thomas C. Cooper

An Owl Book

Henry Holt and Company ❧ New York

Henry Holt and Company, Inc.
Publishers since 1866
115 West 18th Street
New York, New York 10011

Henry Holt® is a registered trademark
of Henry Holt and Company, Inc.

Library of Congress Cataloging-in-Publication Data
Cooper, Thomas C.
Odd lots / Thomas C. Cooper.—1st ed.
p.   cm.
1. Gardening—Massachusetts.   2. Gardens—Massachusetts.
3. Cooper, Thomas C.   I. Title.
SB455.C66   1995   95-7113
635—dc20   CIP

ISBN 0-8050-3741-1
ISBN 0-8050-5026-4 (An Owl Book: pbk.)

Henry Holt books are available for special promotions
and premiums. For details contact: Director, Special Markets.

First published in hardcover in 1995 by
Henry Holt and Company, Inc.

First Owl Book Edition—1996

DESIGNED BY BETTY LEW

Printed in the United States of America
All first editions are printed on acid-free paper.∞

1   3   5   7   9   10   8   6   4   2
1   3   5   7   9   10   8   6   4   2   (pbk.)

These essays appeared in slightly
different form in Horticulture magazine.

For
E.M.B.

Acknowledgments

My thanks to the various editors at *Horticulture* who have worked on these pieces: John Barstow, Tom Fischer, Steve Krauss, and Debbie Starr. Their efforts always brought improvements, and I am grateful for their valuable assistance. Thanks also to Kit Ward, for her enthusiastic support and wise counsel, and to Ray Roberts, for his great interest in making good books.

Contents

Foreword

In the May 1984 issue of *Horticulture* magazine, under the heading "A Note from the Editor," I published a short account of my plans for a new border I was putting in that spring. The piece ran at the front of the issue, and the intention of that essay—and those that have followed in every issue since then—was to capture the world in and around a garden. Because the garden I knew best was my own, the essays shortly evolved into a personal chronicle.

From the start, the essays have been a record of ideas and activities that are for the most part small, even trivial. They make no claim to being practical or profound. They aim to capture the individual, erratic passions of gardeners, as reflected in me and my garden (which I share with my wife, Emily, and our children, Farrar and Nat). Readers have been unwitting bystanders at the birth of my daughter (my son escaped publication), the building of stone walls, my efforts to bring plants into the country from Europe, my pruning and planting habits. They have also had to ride along as we moved house, in the process dismantling one garden and building another from scratch.

Certain subjects occur more than once, though not always in the same season. That is the way of gardening: The same tasks—pruning and weeding, watering and staking—confront the gardener year in and year out. To some people that might seem like drudgery, but not to a gardener. The gardener always relishes having another crack at doing things better. And gardeners are convinced things are getting better in their plot. Though their doubts and misgivings are many, gardeners are in the end optimists, firm believers that the glass is half full. Yet they are happily obsessed by the half that wants filling.

There are two gardens mentioned in these essays: The first was a postage-stamp affair in the middle of Cambridge, Massachusetts. It was an intimate, shady oasis, full of birds and narrow borders stuffed with plants. It had tucks and turns and good architecture—in short, it was all a garden could be, and I will always have a special place for it in my heart.

My present garden, and the one that appears most noticeably in these essays, sits on a rectangle of ground cut into a slope on the outskirts of Boston. The property amounts to a little more than a third of an acre. The house and a small garage (with an attached potting shed) fill two corners of the lot. The remainder is given over to gardens and lawn. Borders enclose the lawn on all sides, amounting in total to more than 300 feet of mixed borders ten to twelve feet deep. There is forty or fifty feet of boxwood hedging, a couple of apple trees, and a kitchen garden. It is a small, simple operation, which, despite our efforts, becomes larger and more complicated with each year.

Keeping this sort of public journal has had the beneficial effect of forcing me to study my place with particular attention. For that I am grateful; otherwise I most likely would rush headlong from one activity to the next, failing to notice the emerging snout of a bulb or the spider web draped between two chamaecyparis. This morning, after the first killing frost of the year, the grasses stood out against the dark green of the arborvitae hedges, and a row of late 'Black-Seeded Simpson' lettuce sparkled against the dew-soaked soil of the kitchen garden. And for the first time I spotted the wasps' nest hanging up in the branches of a Chinese dogwood. The nest was bulbous and ribbed like a Tuscan urn. I must have walked beneath it a hundred times this summer without seeing or hearing it. But there it was this morning, a small reminder of the riches any garden offers throughout the year, no matter its size or location.

ODD LOTS

January

AT THE START OF THE YEAR I CLEAR THE BEDSIDE TABLE of novels and newsmagazines and prepare to settle down with the authors from Park and Burpee, Thompson & Morgan and Jackson & Perkins, Kinsman, Canyon Creek, and White Flower Farm. I am eager to read their predictions for the future of my garden, though I can make a good guess as to how they think things will turn out. No matter how hard the year just past has been or how trying the year ahead looks, the nursery owners forecast a bright future and send out catalogs filled with pictures and words of encouragement. Their voices are strong and cheerful, often jubilant. The weather may be without virtue, the economy may be standing on its head, but the mail-order message that lands on hundreds of thousands of doorsteps is one of undimmed promise. Their prose brims with discoveries large and small, all dressed in superlatives and embroidered with exclamations.

The catalogs themselves arrive without fanfare; one day a single copy appears on the vestibule floor. However, like a snowstorm whose first flakes amount to nothing but build slowly to a thick blanket, the catalogs keep coming, sometimes three or four in a day. I give each a quick look and set it aside on a bench in the front hall. Soon enough they make a pile that threatens to avalanche. With the thought of my inquisitive one-year-old knocked off his feet by the prospects of the coming year, I haul the collection upstairs to the bedroom.

I don't read the catalogs as much as I lay siege to them. Armed with pens, pencils, Post-its, and garden notebooks from past years, I go through them time and again. As items catch my attention, I turn down the corner of the page (though not necessarily for good). With each pass I note new things worth having and reject things from earlier rounds. Any page might have some plants checked in pencil, others circled in pen. There are slashes through some entries, Xs on others. Finally, there are Post-its to signal significant possibilities. The result of all this looks more like a game of tic-tac-toe than a rational decision process. But then, the goal is not simply to decide quickly and finally what needs ordering for the garden.

It is some time before I actually fill out order forms and start writing checks. For the moment I am only choosing plants and seeds, free from the annoyance of budgets or property lines.

Without worry for sunlight or soil type, I select trees and shrubs and herbs and vegetables to add to my garden. When it is filled to even its imaginary limit, I turn to other gardens, adding lily pools and woodland walks to my parents' property, an orchard and a vegetable garden to the neighbors' yard down the street. I wrap a friend's garage in climbing roses and lay a terrace for another friend, ornamenting it with elaborate potted plantings. I tear out ten-foot-tall yews from around her front porch, replace them with *Acer griseum*, and fall asleep exhausted before I can choose a groundcover.

Next month I will get down to the serious work of winnowing the list of items to those that I need for the coming season. But for the moment I am happy to while away the time listening to the siren songs of catalog makers. In the process of gathering, annotating, rejecting, and revising, I have taken up weeks of winter and brought myself happily that much closer to spring.

Living in a coastal town, we can't count on much snow during the course of a winter. Our climate is temperate, even mild, and storms are forever skirting us at the last moment in favor of more rural and mountainous territory. The snow falls elsewhere, and we get only a light dusting of banter from the forecasters. Every once in a long while nature conspires to leave us wallowing. In 1978, twenty-nine inches fell almost overnight, and though the snow receded soon enough, people still talk about the storm with awe and excitement. As a rule, though, only a few feet or so fall each winter and rarely with the fury or singular abundance that the weatherpeople predict. Which all goes to prove that they are not really practicing a science, and, as everyone knows, that we no longer get the big snowstorms we used to get.

After a green and rainy Christmas our new year started with a blast of snow and stormy weather. As if on cue the storm turned north just as it reached us, but we still had snow falling and wind blowing for two days, and when everything stopped I measured six inches outside our front door. Not much, yet deep enough to look and feel like winter proper and to work all the changes you expect from a blanket of snow. Overnight all the ragged edges and stubble of the flower beds disappeared. A smooth and soft coverlet lay across the brown and lumpy soil, the curving shapes of the beds clearly yet softly outlined. A thick layer of icy snow traced the branches of the lilacs, the mock orange, and the dogwood, and a fluffy mound topped a young broom in a carefree way, with a spray of green twigs showing under one corner like the tousled hair sticking out from under a young boy's winter cap. Along the front walk an edging of lavender was squashed to the ground, but after being uncovered it bobbed upright and even managed to give off a slight scent of summer. Nearby a rose stretched its canes along one wall, each branch carrying a thin frosting of white. In the low light of early evening the yard glowed with greater brilliance than a garden of white flowers.

When the snow stopped falling, activity returned to our yard in a hurry. I took up the snow shovel and started working my way along the walks. Two woodpeckers appeared to study a maple tree, and above me in the crown of a pin oak a squirrel began making his way along a limb, off on some errand. He went along briskly, his tail flicking confidently to and fro, but his composure disappeared when he attempted to jump between two limbs. I have seen him make the leap many times and often at greater speed, but this time he was off. He missed his mark on landing and fell five feet or so, unleashing a small avalanche of snow about him as he tumbled through the branches. Somehow he managed to catch a branch, and after pausing for a minute he proceeded on his way more cautiously and with a dusting of snow on his back.

The city garden in winter, bare of its summer finery, often appears threadbare and unappealing. Houses you had forgotten in the summer, when they were invisible behind a curtain of foliage, suddenly reappear closer than before, and the roar of every car for blocks around rings in your ears. A snowstorm brings a reprieve from these sights and sounds. Cars are muffled and looming buildings are made somehow smaller. The snow closes in around you, and everything else moves into the distance. There's never enough, of course, and it disappears all too fast, but that's always the way of things in the garden.

There is little daylight left for a person at this stage of the year once all the business of the day is done. The sun sets shortly after noon it seems, so even on a weekend you need to be up and running early in order to get anything accomplished. Many people would tell you that is just as well, the ground is solid anyway. But a gardener would prove them wrong. You have only to watch one spend a Saturday in winter to understand his talent for whipping up work out of thin air. The metabolism of a gardener may slow in winter, but the vital functions are strong and need only the slightest excuse to spring into action.

At breakfast, for instance, the gardener announces he has nothing to do and will go for a walk before he dies of boredom, whereupon he heads out the door for an inspection of the gardens. Almost immediately he discovers a trowel he left out the last day of planting bulbs. Its blade is frozen deep in the ground, and he spends some time prying it free. He leaves it at the cellar door and goes back to check on some new trees, also planted last fall, to see if they are still wearing their collars of mulch. The mulch looks fine, but he cannot help adjusting it here and there. The plants are blue hollies. He concludes that these particular specimens are not so blue as others he has seen elsewhere and so are more attractive. This conclusion warms him, as does the sun, which has made some progress across the sky. The gardener is even tempted to prune a few shrubs that clearly need attention. With luck he restrains himself (or this day will never end) and does not do now what should most surely be put off until later. Procrastination out of doors is a virtue much admired in gardeners at this time of the year.

During lunch he dreams about grand improvements to the

gardens. Then he takes the rescued trowel down to the cellar, where one thing leads to another, and he spends the next two hours busily oiling and sharpening tools (repeating a job he carried out in November). He moves seven stacks of clay pots across the room. This has no benefit for the pots, but it does allow him to construct a small bench for them. He tries once again to adjust the reel of his push mower so that his lawn will not look like it was cut by a sheep missing half its teeth. He concludes, some forty-five minutes after starting this project, that the mower is seriously out of kilter, may have been so when purchased, and needs the attention of a professional. (Already the list for next weekend's work is under way.)

By the time the gardener finishes his work in the cellar, the sun has fallen below the horizon, and the wind is up and rustling. He decides to postpone overseeding the section of lawn that looks so dingy. Instead, he goes upstairs and records the day's activities in his garden journal, or if he lacks a journal he gives an account to anyone willing to listen. After dinner he settles down with the latest catalogs. The evening wears on, and he goes to bed with a book—on irises, say—and falls asleep with it propped against his nose, his thoughts full of spring, when he will be rid of this season of inactivity and back at work in the garden.

I am in the process of training two modest myrtle plants into standards, and I am coming to the conclusion it would be easier to train two young boys to sit still in their seats during dinner. Whenever I forget to give the myrtles their constitutional quarter-turn, they promptly bend their leaders this way or that. They are quickly taking on the appearance of bowlegged twins, which is not how they looked when I bought them. Being tightly potted they need constant attention with the watering can as well. So far they are merely gaining height, with little or no attention given to their ultimate character. They look more like bushy bean poles than the statuesque centerpieces I hope they will become.

It doesn't seem as though it should take terribly long to establish a collection of houseplants, certainly nothing near the time needed for an outdoor garden. The garden outside is larger—usually much larger—and more unruly, with animals and weather besetting you on all sides. All the same, the occasional successes I have enjoyed outdoors have not been matched in the house. Plants of all persuasions have passed through our house, and most have ended life on the compost heap, shriveled testaments to my fickle treatment.

There have been some bright spots now and then. I have coaxed a number of camellias into bloom, although for a while they seemed determined to drop their buds at the last moment, and one particular favorite, a plant whose name I can't remember, bloomed exuberantly one year and died immediately afterward. One of the most common and most durable of my small collection is a *Ficus lyrata* that came to me with one withered leaf and a rotting root ball. I pruned off the leaf and much of the root ball, and to my surprise the plant survived. Seven years later it remains a small plant, but it continues to put forth new floppy leaves. I cherish it for its tenacity and dream that it may grow big enough to rival an enormous specimen I once saw in California, with leaves truly the size of an elephant's ear and a thick, contorted trunk that twisted and turned to the ceiling.

Far less venerable but nonetheless an essential part of our indoor garden are the bulbs that dot the tabletops and windowsills from December to March. You can count on finding a number of amaryllises as well as pots and pans full of paperwhites. Beyond those staples you might come across most any bulb. This year there are numerous tulips and hyacinths. They never quite made it into the ground before the frost arrived, so I potted them up and stashed them on the stairs beneath the cellar hatch. Given the squirrels' ransacking of the new bulbs this fall, it may be the best possible outcome.

None of these plants was chosen for its part in a plan, a design such as you would attempt outdoors. I bought plants I admired for their bloom or their form or the fragrance of their flowers. Where they go depends upon the plants' needs and our available space. I can't see that anything is lost by this approach. In the somber, mostly gray months of winter the sight of green leaves and richly colored flowers—to say nothing of the scent of a heliotrope or a jasmine—is reason enough for having them.

The constitution of a gardener is a mercurial mixture of imagination and optimism. Nothing matches it except perhaps the temperament of a young child. Gardeners are endlessly enthusiastic, easily distracted from one passion to another. Set a crisp new catalog before a gardener, or send him a warm, sunny day in May, and he will do most anything except what he intended to do. The following resolutions are, therefore, offered with the understanding that they will be forgotten as soon as the first snowdrop begins to bloom.

Stop accepting plants as gifts, no matter how tempting the offers. In May, friends with good intentions and too many plants come around, supposedly to look at your garden, and pass on a small snippet of a favorite plant. No doubt they like this plant partly because it grows so damn well in their garden with so little trouble. It will surely do the same in your garden. But you've already got plenty to watch over—too much, in fact—so just imagine they are offering a tray of zucchini seedlings.

In early fall round up all the tools and put them away in a safe place. Otherwise your fancy new trowel—or some similar item—will appear next spring under the leaves you never got around to raking. It will look much less fancy. So, for that matter, will the lawn under those leaves.

Take some pictures of your garden every few weeks. That way you will have a record of your efforts and won't need to rely on your memory, which hasn't told the truth in years. Come next January you will avoid buying plants you already have, to put in places where there are already plants (to say nothing of the bulbs).

Have the conviction to throw out your 'Paper-White' narcissus once they pass their peak. They smell wonderful at their best and something on the dark side of musky at their worst. Poinsettias deserve the same treatment. There is nothing wrong with throwing out plants.

Tie up and otherwise support all the plants that need such help. Otherwise you will find yourself either trying in vain to prop up waterlogged delphiniums or lying on the ground to admire them. (I intend to devise some buttress for a spirea that always sags to the ground after early summer rains and flattens a stand of Japanese irises.)

Plan your summer vacation for September or October, not July or August. If you insist on taking a vacation in midsummer, stay at home. There's plenty to do in the garden: diseases to battle, plants to water, weeds to root out, vegetables to pick and freeze, flowers to deadhead. Neglect all this for two weeks and the place will look like a derelict farm (as it did last summer). You'll miss the climbing roses, the best raspberries, the phlox. And you'll ruin a perfectly good friendship with the person you ask to tend the place.

Cultivate the birds in your neighborhood. They depend on you for food and drink, in return for which they animate the garden through the winter with their swooping (the jays) and chatter (the chickadees). The bright red of a cardinal sitting in an evergreen is a sight worth the trip to the feeder in even the worst weather.

Finally, buy some cut flowers every Friday. This is the custom in many other parts of the world and should be here.

I don't go out in the garden much in the dead of winter, but I do keep a constant eye on it. I study it mostly in the morning, since the only light available when I get home is cast by street-lights and it does nothing to improve the profile of tree or shrub. In the early morning the light is low and weak—not sufficient to expose the flaws of the season, but enough to reveal the simple lines of the place.

We don't have a winter garden, in the finest, bookworthy sense of the term. We don't go out on New Year's Day and take inventory of the plants in bloom. Some of the brightest color comes from an orange kickball lodged at the base of hydrangea. Nevertheless, we do manage to find color and scenes that hold our attention.

My day begins with a tour of the garden from the vantage point of the kitchen windows. I look first to the dogwood, the weeping katsura, and the witch hazel, which stand next to one another in the middle of an island border. The dogwood spreads its branches wide in orderly layers, while the witch hazel throws its own out in an upward sweep; the katsura rises up then spills to the ground in a broad fountain. Unlike the conifers, which soak up light and present a dense and dark demeanor, this trio is full of lively character. Their pale gray trunks stand out in the low light, and their spidery branches have an animated character that lightens the heaviness of the season.

Tucked under the outstretched branches of witch hazel is another plant that glimmers early in the day. *Calamagrostis* 'Karl Foerster' is a slender, wispy grass. Above a shaggy mop of leaves it sends up a spire of flower stalks that turn a bright tawny hue and stand ramrod straight through the battering of winter. I like this grass best of all, though the billowing appearance of *Miscanthus sinensis* 'Morning Light'—a straw version of a fountain frozen at the top of its gush—is also a cheering sight.

The most noticeable trunks in the garden, now and in summer, are the pale poles of the pergola, which overlooks the vegetable garden. The pergola is made of locust wood and rises to a peak at fourteen feet. Perhaps because it catches the first rays of sun, it is the park bench of choice for a collection of local birds—a gathering of mostly sparrows and a few crows, whose dark and sharp visages echo the season.

Although the garden in winter is mostly a cross-hatching of yew and boxwood hedges, and spires of conifer and grass, it does contain occasional spots of color. The fiery red berries of the deciduous holly, *Ilex* 'Sparkleberry', last well into the winter, not exciting the birds as much as they do me. Echoing the holly berries are the cardinals that come to visit. When our luck is good we have two pairs in residence through the winter. They like to perch in the holly or on the boxwood hedge that ends next to the feeder. Throughout the day they pass back and forth, making a moveable feast for the color-starved gardener.

In another six weeks there will be daphnes, hellebores, and the signs of early bulbs that the squirrels did not discover. Then I will find myself outside in the mornings clutching a cup of coffee, sniffing and studying the garden (and gathering up the orange kickball). For now, however, I am content with the quiet presence of these plants, simple markers of the dormant garden in winter.

January is a good month for a gardener to state his resolve. Any month will do, because gardeners are constantly hatching new plans and revising old ones. But in this region January is a particularly sensible time to take stock and plan for the new year, as the weather doesn't allow for much other activity. You could argue that the best time is in spring, when gardeners need resolve and restraint in large doses; or maybe the best time is fall, when the flaws and excesses of the season are clear in memory. Still, for people who don't own a greenhouse or live in California (where one month acts pretty much like any other and it's hard to find a minute, let alone a month, to take stock), January makes the most sense.

It's hard to know where to begin with resolutions, but if I hope to accomplish anything the first one should be to take the phone off the hook for most of the sunny weekends from April to October. People who discover I have a more than passing interest in gardening tend to call as soon as I get to the top of a delicately placed ladder and fully tangled in an unruly climbing rose. Friends want to ask any sort of question: Is now a good time to move a certain plant? It has big leaves. Or could I offer some ideas for planting the backyard (but not roses, daylilies, or irises)? I relish the challenge of fashioning answers from my grab bag of gardening knowledge. However, I'm doubtful whether I've improved the quality of anyone's horticulture. And it's often Sunday before I return to the ladder and the roses.

This year I also intend to act more decisively in the matter of self-sowing plants. It's hard to dislike a plant that spreads itself around, adding to the mix that makes a good garden. But there is only so much *Geranium endressii* one person can handle. And if you have a small garden but a large number of plants of this character, you need a harder heart when it comes to pulling seedlings that appear in the midst of your *Asarum*. I turned my head on a small scattering of *Malva alcea* shoots; by the end of the summer they had swamped one end of a border and were setting seeds at a fierce rate. I can't imagine what this year will bring. The same is true of a bed of *Myosotis*, a gift from a neighbor. The young plants lagged most of the spring but gained vigor through the summer and bloomed into November. Such vigor scares me, and next year I won't be taken in by a delicate bloom.

I'll also pay no attention to the instructions on bags of lawn fertilizer. Four years ago I followed their advice about spreader settings and rates of application. It nearly killed the lawn. Last fall I cut the rate in half, and, once again, the lawn looked worse after my attentions than before. This year I will do away with the fertilizer and simply circle the yard with the empty spreader—the dry martini approach to lawn care.

I should get some oil and dip the feet and swab the shoulders of the two benches, which sit outside all winter and now look arthritic. I'll definitely move the bird feeder hanging from the hemlock branch to a more open spot so the birds can eat in more cheerful surroundings. I'll buy no more furniture or pots or peonies, but what plants I do buy I'll send for early instead of phoning in my order in April. That should give me something to do this month.

Having put the garden to bed for the winter, I find there is almost no chance to relax. A new bird feeder stands in the garden, and the activity resembles O'Hare Airport on a busy day. What with studying the comings and goings and making sure the hopper is full of seed (gray-striped sunflower seeds, a particular favorite of the timid and choosy cardinals, which are a particular favorite of my daughter's and mine), there is little time for the rest of the world. The feeder is nothing special, a ranch-style affair painted chocolate brown. A simple counterbalance arrangement keeps birds above a certain weight from getting at the food. Blue jays and other thugs thus cannot monopolize the feeding tray. The jays try all the same, arriving grandly, fluttering their blue-and-white frock coats, and complaining loudly that their exclusion is mean and unreasonable treatment.

The jays are not the biggest problem, though; that honor belongs to the squirrels, which will do anything to get a meal on the cheap. We once had a nice wooden feeder. I suspended it on a long, thin wire from a tree branch, hoping to keep the squirrels at bay. They scoffed at this effort and simply dropped from the branch, crashing onto the feeder and clinging to it for dear life. Once a squirrel had regained its breath, it would hang by its toes from the roof of the feeder and feast with an air that suggested squirrels eat upside down all the time. After a few days I noticed teeth marks in the wood; later I found a hole through one wall. Before long I discarded the feeder.

Having spent considerable time and effort discouraging the attention of squirrels, I was surprised to come across a catalog that offers food and toys for these animals. The Wild Bird Company proposes that we celebrate the persistence and acrobatic qualities of the squirrel. The company offers, for example, a pinwheel arrangement that has three arms; on the end of each arm you stick a corncob. The rig is mounted on a tree or the railing of a deck, and the squirrels go round and round driven by their weight and relentless appetite. You can buy more elaborate whirligigs as well, or a squirrel seesaw. If you prefer to create your own games, you can order a bag of corncobs or a specially formulated mixture of seeds and nutritional supplements ("calcium, alfalfa, pellets, etc."). There is also a section of books about the exploits of squirrels and chipmunks. It seems a schizophrenic approach, hawking squirrel-proof feeders on one page and snacks and toys for squirrels on the next. It reminds me more of a foreign relations policy than a direct-mail sales pitch.

So far my new feeder is keeping the squirrels from the birds, but I know from reading about bird feeders that I face other foes. If the seed gets wet, parasites may crop up and endanger all the birds who innocently accept my hospitality. There is also the danger of the neighborhood cats, who care nothing for sunflower seeds but would love to catch a bird. Imagine the risk to a bird if I installed a seesaw—the distraction of a rollicking squirrel might allow a cat to sneak up and nab an otherwise wary chickadee. Although the plants may be resting, there is plenty for the gardener to keep an eye on in the winter—the beauty of the cautious cardinal and greed of the selfish squirrel.

I calculate that over the course of a year I spend roughly sixty hours simply looking at my garden and its plants. That works out to something more than ten minutes a day, on average. I have never exactly kept track of these minutes, but I know there have been countless times when I have stood looking at something long enough to let a cup of coffee go cool or a glass of wine grow warm. As I say, this number accounts strictly for simple gazing, though that does not mean the time is spent idly or that it is wasted. I am hard at work, trying to unravel the secrets of the plants and the garden, to clear up problems and answer questions of the sort that keeps gardeners awake in the middle of the night. These are not the sort of questions that torment tax attorneys and politicians.

In summer there are enough things to ponder that I often wake at the crack of dawn to get on with these debates. Yet invariably I end the morning with a list of "Things to Think About" that is longer than the one I had when I got out of bed. Usually I begin the day peering out from the kitchen, but it isn't long before some planting, real or imagined, demands closer look, and I am off for heated conversation with myself about design and cultural matters. Do the rodgersias really belong next to the kirengeshoma, and why is one so vigorous and the other so poky? Is 'Blue Queen' the right salvia next to *Achillea* 'Moonshine'? Is there too much gray foliage along the walk or not enough? Often I can have the same debate three or four days running and reach four or five different conclusions. Probably I should carry a notebook, but then I would spend less time studying the garden and too much time scribbling notes, which are better made at night when your head is cooler and less full of ideas.

With the garden reduced to its skeleton in winter there is just as much to look at and stew about. The ivies emerge from a summer cloaked by other plants and show themselves against walls and fences. The deciduous hollies, bland and unnoticed in summer, are jeweled now. Should we have more of them? Perhaps that would improve our bird population. Then maybe we need more birdhouses and feeders, but where to put them, to best help the birds and the garden? Unhindered by the annoyance of all the plants that in summer crowd the ground, the garden is replanted and rearranged morning after morning through the winter. Hedges are installed and brought to perfection in a moment. One morning I wrapped the vegetable garden with a low, gnarled cordon of pears before even finishing the first cup of coffee.

During the last year I have devoted a lot of thought to a motley assembly of conifers loitering against the front of our house. They are overgrown and battling one another. All but a few need to be removed. But just what should replace them and in what order has kept me staring at the front of the house for hours. The neighbors may wonder if I am thinking of painting the place or changing the window arrangement. Or maybe they imagine I have been locked out of the house—and if so, why. But I am only lost in thought over the countless options. It is this never-ending process of evaluation that makes gardening so maddening and so thrilling. A garden is never so good as it will be next year and yet it is never so bad that the imagination and a steady gaze cannot find in it bits of beauty and possibility.

This year began like all others, with the sound of spring catalogs dropping through the mail slot. Most years I let them lie there for a few weeks, ripening, while my feelings for winter go sour. But this year I was on the alert for them and got right down to reading. The reason is that I intend to order a pair of matched lilacs for my nephew. He is not a gardener; he is only a young boy closing in on four who spends most of his time outdoors, which is where children and lilacs are at their best.

The lilac's personality is no longer so straightforward as it once was. Those people who believe that any good thing must be improved and cloned at any cost—the sort of folks who bring you basketball in June and football in July—are working the same tricks on the scent and season of the lowly lilac. The flower is no longer a beacon of spring. Arching sprays of lilac blooms now nod from almost every florist's window throughout the fall and winter. They look oddly out of place to me, and I can detect none of the familiar fragrance. If it is a fragrance you are after, however, pay no attention to these blooms. Stop in at your local emporium and buy a bar of lilac soap, a canister of talc, or some perfume. You can wash your hands in lilac, take a bath in it, dust off or oil up with it; and if that doesn't satisfy your nose, you can douse the air with lilac-scented aerosol spray. Some people will surely decide that this new, improved, designer lilac fits perfectly in their midwinter arrangements, but I find it doesn't fit at all with my idea of how a spring-flowering shrub ought to behave or be treated.

I grew up with quite another lilac. It goes by the name of common lilac (*Syringa vulgaris*). It is called common, I think, in the same way that some people are said to have common sense or common looks. Though reasonably attractive, the plant is not extravagant in posture or foliage. In bloom, it offers a distinctive but quiet perfume. Quiet and, for me, unmistakable—a smell that signals the arrival of true spring (as opposed to the earlier portion of spring, which is little more than a cover-up for mud season and the lingering snowstorms of winter). Even now that I live in milder surroundings, a place with a long and luxurious spring, I hold off until the lilacs are in full bloom before putting my boots on the shelf.

If I had room for a separate spring garden, it would include a hedge of common lilac. The smell of lilac is the earliest one I can remember, one whose annual return brings with it associations as clear and rich as the scent itself. The role of smell is an aspect of garden design that gets little attention, which is too bad. The plants will pass, the garden will grow over, but let the scent reappear, anywhere, and the garden is rebuilt. My nephew may never learn to like a hoe, but once acquainted with the smell from a hedge of lilacs in spring, he will know a good deal about the addiction that people feel for plants.

Sometime around now we usually get a stretch of warm weather. It doesn't always appear in January; some years it doesn't appear at all. But most years a spell of unusually warm days occurs between January and March, and over time people have come to call this deviant stretch the January thaw. The symptoms are almost always the same: The temperature soars, the snow melts, and people go around shaking their heads. Most people, I imagine, greet this thaw with a mixture of pleasure and apprehension. On the one hand, a break of warm temperatures is always welcome; on the other, there is a suspicion that it signals a flaw in the proper state of nature. Many people consider the thaw a cruel joke sent by an angry god. Tell one of these folks that it's nice to have a few good days and he will assure you that we will pay for it.

Gardeners view the January thaw with dread. A spell of mild weather followed (inevitably) by a freeze is a recipe for disaster. The strain of such a roller coaster on a plant's system is often killing, and some plants are simply ripped (or heaved, depending on which side of the argument you take) out of the ground.

A constant covering of snow is the simple solution, of course, and it is what all northern gardeners hope for. Beneath a layer of snow the temperature remains constant and up to seventy degrees warmer than the air temperature. Given a thick quilt of snow, gardeners need not worry about gathering up tons of evergreen boughs to arrange over their perennial beds. But sadly, the snow comes and goes when we least expect it, arriving too late one year, disappearing too early another, and in some winters never really coming at all.

You cannot count on snow, but that is no reason not to like it. Snow offers much more to the gardener than protection against the cold. Overnight a snowfall changes a garden from a forlorn wasteland to a landscape of clean, soft lines and stark contrasts. All scars, all chores left undone, and unfortunately all tools left uncollected, are hidden from sight. Lawn and borders disappear, obliterated except for hints of their outlines indicated by slight depressions in the snow. Lawn, trees, shrubs, walks, and walls alike are draped in a soft covering of white, reducing the garden to an arrangement of shapes and forms.

The perfection of this scene is quickly undone. Shoveling reveals the walks; dogs, cats, and children crisscross the lawn. The snow gradually loses its perfect, smooth whiteness and turns lumpy and mottled, taking on the aspect of a sea of mashed potatoes rather than a perfectly plumped down pillow. And then, without fail, there comes the thaw, reducing the snow altogether, leaving only a few lonely graying mounds in shaded spots.

This year the January thaw arrived early, just as the month

started. It returned the garden to its barren, wintry appearance. The temperature rose into the forties, and birds appeared to prospect on the lawn with fresh enthusiasm. I came across a bulb planter left abandoned at the end of planting last fall. It was a welcome reminder of the treasures beneath the frozen beds awaiting for a real spring to arrive.

FEBRUARY

THE PROPRIETOR OF A SMALL CITY GARDEN, OF A SIZE
that can be circled without ever getting beyond the call of the
kitchen phone or being away so long that the coffee grows cold,
is lucky when it comes to the matter of sound in the garden. I
know that many people will tell you, if you ask them, that the
city gardener is a sad creature, battered by obnoxious and
never-ending noise: planes overhead, cars on either flank, and
all around dogs bent on warning someone about something.
There is no quiet, the critics claim. And they will go on to
inform you (without needing any prompting) that a place in
the country, on the contrary, is rich with glorious silence.

I won't deny that a person in the country enjoys some wonderful sounds (though what these people—myself included—

hanker for is not really silence but enough quiet to hear the things we like). The evening song of the spring peepers, for instance, is a thrilling chorus that I doubt I shall ever hear from my current backyard. The sound of a brook is clearly out of the question.

Still, we of the inner city are not abandoned by Nature. The rain falls here, and you have only to plant some ornamental grass and soon the wind will come around to wrestle with it. But the city sounds I enjoy most are not those made by the garden but rather those created by the gardener. Here the city dweller excels, in many instances because the small scope of his activities encourages him to use instruments that, on a larger site, turn a simple task into a tedious one. The refrain from these hand-powered tools is captivating, satisfying. The sound of hedge clippers, say, the crisp, metallic bark they make as they scissor through green privet shoots. I like listening to the rise and fall of a push-reel mower's music, knowing from the pitch and rhythm whether its operator is striding purposefully across an open stretch, turning a corner, or scooting in under the lower leaves of sprawling yew. There is a satisfaction in making this music to your liking—fast and crisp or lazy and rolling; and when you stop to rest, happily there is no lingering racket to remind you that time is wasting and you had better hop to.

Even at this gray and quiet time of year, my garden is not silent. Indeed, one of my favorite sounds is at its best in this season. It is a small wind chime, brought from China by my neighbors Amy and Philip and now hanging in the branches of a gnarled hydrangea outside the dining room. I wish I could claim credit for the tune; sadly I can't. It is really an agreeable collaboration: I provide the chime, Mother Nature brings the wind. The sound is nothing exotic, just a light, clear melody played whenever there's a breeze on the block. The notes carry easily in the dry winter air, and I find that on this small plot they substitute wonderfully for a brook out back.

Proponents of the good old days find fault with the modern era wherever they look. The railroads aren't worth a dime (and neither is a dime). There is no music worth listening to, and there hasn't been good poetry written since Shakespeare's sonnets. And at this time of the year the northern members of this loose society grow wistful about the weather. The snows, they claim, are not as deep or as frequent as they used to be.

Having grown up in Vermont, I share this complaint about the quality and quantity of modern snowfalls. My recollections is of winters smothered in snow—snowdrifts lapping at the kitchen windowsills and walls of it thrown up along the roadsides by plows. We built vast forts in these bankings, complete with caves and lengthy tunnels. It may be that the introduction of salt has put an end to great and lasting piles along the roads, but we never seem to have as much snow these days.

According to the folks at the National Oceanic and Atmospheric Administration, this nostalgic grousing is well founded. From 1915 to 1975 the Boston area received an average of 40.5 inches of snowfall each winter. However, since

1975 the actual annual snowfall has decreased. Between 1980 and 1985 the average was down to 37 inches; between 1985 and 1990 that number dropped to 31 inches. Furthermore, the number of storms leaving six or more inches of snow in the last twenty years has decreased by 27 percent as compared with the previous twenty-year period. The only good news for snow lovers is that dust in the atmosphere, left over from volcanoes in places such as the Philippines and Alaska, may cool the air enough to give us greater than normal snowfalls.

Had I heard this prediction earlier, I might have made the effort last winter to protect my two *Chamaecyparis lawsoniana* 'Ellwoodii' with a wrapping of twine. As it was, the first real storm of the winter caught us off guard (and out of town) and flattened not only the chamaecyparis but almost everything else in the garden, including an old twenty-foot-high crab apple. We returned home in the early evening on December 13 to find the garden buried beneath a foot and a half of wet snow. The seven-foot-tall hedge of arborvitae was half that height; the other conifers, the hollies, the daphnes, and the witch hazel were bent to the ground.

I plodded around the dark and eerily quiet garden, the snow still falling lightly. The formless quality of the landscape was disorienting; it was suddenly necessary to check my bearings. At one point I stepped on a *Pinus parviflora* 'Brevifolia', and minutes later I tripped over the crumpled remains of zebra grass. Most of the trees and shrubs were bowed but unbroken; in the following week they regained their former shapes. The conifers, however, remained stooped in the bent postures of old men. Some other plants suffered more. A stately, ten-foot-tall 'Montbatten' juniper had broken in two; five old and twisted lilacs had snapped at head height, as did one trunk of a Chinese dogwood.

Come spring I will replace the juniper and begin the process of rejuvenating the lilacs. In a couple years the garden will show no signs of this storm, and in a few more years I will forget it ever occurred. But for the moment I am somehow glad for this reminder that nature is neither orderly nor predictable, and that, no matter what the averages, we still occasionally get snowstorms like the old ones.

Needing a reason to keep me from the temptations of spring catalogs, I have lately been sorting through bundles of photographs I took during the course of last year. Not all the pictures are in focus, but certain lessons come clear after shuffling through only a few packets. Right away it's obvious that there are far too many pictures of other gardens and equally few of the garden in my backyard. The regrettable fact is that gardeners garden and photographers take photographs, and the two personalities rarely get along, despite the finest intentions of many gardeners. When the gardener ought to get a camera and photograph some plant—his prize delphinium looking its best in five years, say—there is usually not time for such a frivolous errand. Taking a picture will involve changing dirt-caked shoes, washing dirt-caked hands, and rummaging in the closet for the camera. All this when there is work to be done. And if he does decide to drop everything, the gardener, whose eyes function equally (if not perfectly) well under all conditions, is at the mercy of his camera, which works poorly except in thinly overcast light and the absence of wind. Sooner or later, I imagine, many folks give up the idea of taking beautiful photographs of their garden, preferring to catch a few shots on the run, saying to themselves, "Well, I'll just take a picture of that phlox for the records." They may secretly hope for more, but they won't say so.

Outside his own yard, a gardener with a camera behaves quite differently. His quixotic pursuit of the perfect picture is endless. Around each corner, down every path, is a sight to behold, and after each shot there is a rush for the next vista. The product of this frenzy is a great stack of slides or prints bound to lie listless for years until they are thinned to a slim sampling.

The pictures that are kept need not be beautiful by any means. Like pictures of one's children, their beauty lies in the memory they hold for the photographer. It may be a particular scene in a garden that seemed worth duplicating, or some stubby little sprouts on their way to becoming plants. People may be beheaded, the world may tilt dangerously. No matter, for like the often oddly colored photographs in the spring catalogs, it is the hint of promise that's all-important.

A garden changes little in winter. If you put aside the matters of foliage and flowers, and overlook the lawn (which is often best overlooked anyway), the garden remains as it was in summer. So a person ought to draw his plans with winter as well as summer in mind. A garden that is attractive in winter will almost certainly be a pleasure in summer, though the reverse is not often true.

There is little reason for venturing out at this time of year. Still, I am thankful for the paths and steps that have gradually accumulated throughout our garden. A hodgepodge of paving stones edges all the beds. I originally installed them to give certain plants a place to loll without smothering the lawn or getting chewed up by the mower. I think these stones make their best impression in winter; the slightly meandering line they follow looks surprisingly graceful, and with no plants wanting your attention, there is time to admire this outline. Elsewhere old bricks, unearthed as we dug various parts of the garden and stood on end to make a slightly raised bed, suggest order and permanence in the otherwise ragged and all-too-seasonal garden. Their mossy tops and rusty tone add a bit of winter color. The latest addition to our winter garden is a long stretch of fence that bounds two sides of the yard. It is a simple structure, butted boards with a small cap running along the top, and the whole thing left to weather naturally. The strong and regular lines of this fence (which replaced a teetering chain version) provide height and mass in a garden now void of such things.

Actually, the place is not entirely without these qualities. There is a young crab apple in one corner. We planted it with the idea that its leaves will in time screen out a nearby utility pole and the power lines that converge at its top. Without leaves the crab apple gives no protection against the view, but its branches hang heavily with clusters of dark-red fruits, which are ample distraction from the pole and its wires. (The same good words must be said about the small, gemlike fruits of the hollies, which keep their leaves, to boot.) I cannot claim as much admiration for the lilacs that are numerous around the place. They look awkward and gangly when stripped of their leaves. As a justification for keeping them, I hang bird feeders off their branches. This arrangement suits the birds fine and makes something worthwhile of these spring bloomers.

Even some of the summer-loving plants play a part in giving this garden a life in winter. The spires of astilbe, especially the tall ones such as *A. tacquetii* 'Superba', stand erect through the winter, as do the cattail spikes of liatris and the loosestrife. Not so the withered and brown leaves of Siberian and Japanese irises; they flop to the ground with the first frosts, if not sooner. The sight of the tousled leaves weaving a rumpled carpet across the ground may not excite others, but it reminds me of the tawny-hued salt marshes I once lived beside, which is reason enough to spare them during fall cleanup.

It don't know that I'll ever build a garden strictly for the winter. There are three other seasons to contend with, and lots of plants and even more ideas that don't take well to cold and snow. But I am thankful for the parts of my garden that give it interest and character at this turn of the year.

Much as we try to attract birds to our garden, they come and go without apparent regard for our invitations. This may be due to the irregularity of our feeding schedule or the type of food or maybe the design of the feeders. The brazen behavior of local squirrels must also affect the birds' visits. No doubt there are other factors I can't imagine. I am only happy that they stop in with such good frequency.

Although our lot is small and solidly in the city, we are reasonably well set up for birds. We have six good-size trees with perches of all sorts. A flock of sparrows can turn in for a morning and every one can find a seat with steady footing and good views. A dense and shadowy stand of hemlocks offers privacy for the more reclusive birds and acts as a shield against wind, rain, and snow for those caught out without a jacket. There are assorted shrubs, evergreen and otherwise, but only a tangled mock orange, a sprawling viburnum, and a common burning bush attract much interest from the birds. A modest piece of lawn acts as a landing field, a promenade for courting, and, most important, a rich source of worms.

Beyond plucking worms from the lawn, the birds don't forage much in our garden. They avoid the rose hips. Crimson-colored crab apples shrivel and blacken on the limbs without so much as a single taker. Holly berries go untouched through even the hardest winter. The reluctance to try our natural offering may be characteristic of suburban birds. More probably it is a simple result of the number of bird feeders around the place that provide food without the need for picking it or cleaning the seeds.

This preference suits us fine, for we are flush with feeders. At last count we had five set up around the garden. They range from the traditional hutch with glass walls to a more modern contraption with two plastic bowls connected by a metal rod. In one lilac there is a small terra-cotta feeder shaped like a water droplet turned upside down, with a short perch the size of a well-worn pencil. For Christmas this year a friend sent us another ceramic feeder. This one is considerably larger and roughly resembles a silo. None of them is at all squirrel-proof—though the makers claim otherwise—so you are just as likely to look out the window and find a slovenly gray squirrel gorging himself as a stately cardinal. I much prefer the cardinal; however, there is some pleasure in watching a squirrel stuff himself while hanging by his feet from a slippery metal rod. Given the constant adjustments required to maintain their footing and the nervous energy expended watching for signs of danger, I doubt the squirrels are getting fat at our feeders.

The squirrels will eat most anything, but the birds are another matter. We have tried three types of food without finding one that all of them enjoy. One mixture they rejected unanimously, another seemed to suit all but the cardinals. We now buy a mix approved by the Audubon Society, and though the winter is young, our offering appears to meet with general approval.

We did not make this garden with the goal of attracting birds, as some people do. Birds call on us all the same. A full assortment of common characters—jays, cardinals, sparrows, chickadees, robins—pass through. Even a seagull shows up occasionally, looking uncomfortable on such solid ground. And in the dead of winter with so little color and so little life visible in the garden, it's a welcome treat to have the visitors.

In the far northern parts of this country winter begins so early and continues so long that there is barely time for a breath of summer before another winter closes in. The hard edge of winter often cuts down the blooms and bounty of summer shortly after Labor Day, laying siege to the land until May and retreating then only grudgingly. There is a harshness about these winters that makes winter in Boston seem kind and forgiving, almost tropical. But the landscapes they create are not without beauty, of a sort so spare and delicate it is a lesson to gardeners from more temperate parts of the country.

Every winter I visit a town in the upper reaches of the Adirondacks in New York State, two hours north of Albany. The highest mountain peaks are close by, and the Hudson River at this stage of its journey to Manhattan is a boulder-strewn stream narrow enough to skip a rock across. There are conifers in great numbers clustered in dense stands.

Under a deep cover of snow, the land is virtually without edges. The dips and rolls of the ground that show themselves so clearly in summer now disappear in this seamless scene. The snow hides all, improves all. Beneath its mantle of snow, a battered trash can takes on a certain regal beauty. Craggy boulders become white haystacks, and a pair of ski tracks or footprints give distinction to an otherwise formless field. The view becomes two-dimensional and oddly without scope, at once both vast and minute. The pines, spruces, firs, and junipers provide depth and a sense of scale. They seem perfectly at home in this climate, not the dark funereal masses they often become in the gardens of more mild climate, but the perfect black contrast to a white world. They form sharp spires and broad pyramids that stand out against the soft snow-covered ground, and one need not touch them to know they are needled and rough-textured.

The adolescent leaves of beech trees rustle in the wind; they add a lone bit of parched golden-brown color. Small wispy clumps of goldenrod, asters, and other summer-blooming natives poke above the snow. In protected nooks of houses, willowy stalks of hydrangeas and heliopsis stand as gaunt reminders of modest summer gardens, a few remaining florets dangling lifelessly in the cold air. Hoary canes of rugosa roses bristle in the winter wind. These small details look even more pale against the backdrop of conifers and mountains, their color bleached by the overriding black and white. Still, they stand out sharply on the snow-covered ground.

When it snows, as it often does, the world goes from black and white to one of muted grays, at once delicate and indistinct. One is aware of the simplest lines and shapes and forms. Even without color and great tangles of foliage, there is still plenty to see. Walking in this snowy landscape, I am reminded of the temple gardens of the Orient and of gardens I have seen in southern California and the Southwest, where a single palm trunk against a stucco wall or a stone set in a place of sand created a similarly satisfying composition. I am not tempted to create a Japanese garden, nor do I wish for a longer and harder winter, but I relish their simple elegance, their ability to make much from little, to turn an inhospitable world into one of beauty.

Even the most housebound, winter-congested nose has no trouble picking up the scent of the winter-blooming narcissus. It might fail to notice a freesia, or even overlook a hyacinth, but *Narcissus tazetta* is unavoidable. The form of this bulb is that most people know is called 'Paper-White'. First, seduced by the smell, they go overboard and allow too many to flower at once. Unless you live in a castle or a particularly drafty house, there's little need for more than two or three pots at any one time. Five or six pots in full flower will give a normal home the nauseating air of a cheap-perfume outlet. Second, people often wait too long before throwing out their bulbs, allowing the raw taint of decay to seep into the rich perfume of the 'Paper-White'. Each year I grow about four dozen of these Mediterranean natives, generally aiming to have two pots in flower through January and February. The exception to this rule is Christmastime, a season when excess is the order of the land. For Christmas I have a couple of extra pots on hand to compete with noses overwhelmed by eggnog, swags of juniper, and balsam boughs. Otherwise I pot up the bulbs in batches of three, four, and six. By the time the last container has gone to the compost pile, I have tired of the scene, and there are other perfumes to sample.

A recent addition to our winter garden is *Viburnum ×bodnantense* 'Dawn'. This is not a plant to grow for great grace. You plant it where its stocky, somewhat ungainly looks are hidden in summer. Then you wait until winter, when the stubby branches provide a shy but regular show of light-pink blooms. The flowers are small and their fragrance delicate, but in the clear air of winter the scent carries well. You can cut some branches and let them bloom indoors as well. A handful of stems stuck in a vase will take the chill off a room. And the stems themselves, which branch at right angles to the main trunk, have a look of strength and fortitude that one often needs in the depths of winter.

One can also take comfort in the looks of the witch hazel, which is both strong and graceful. Ours is the first plant you see from our kitchen door, and its broad vase shape is always a treat—especially in winter when the ground around it is bare and the birds use it as a clubhouse. When no birds are about, I snip branches to fill a pitcher. It goes on the kitchen table, where we can watch the dark nuggets of bud unfurl into pale-yellow tassels and debate the qualities of their spicy perfume.

When there are no flowers to sniff, there are always the pungent leaves of scented geranium (lemon, in our case) to crush. I also like to run my hands over the bristly head of a standard rosemary, releasing its aroma and taking a dose away with me on my hands. And this year we added to our collection a savory, *Satureia vinimea*, whose lime-green leaves strike my nose as minty. None of these has the power of a 'Paper-White'—very few do—but they all are harbingers of the daphnes, the roses, and the other viburnums that will shortly bloom outside.

For the gardener whose land is locked in frost and whose spirits are dark and uneasy, the bulbs of winter are talismans of strong magic and hope. There are many plants, of course, that one can raise indoors to ward off the chill of desolation and desperation, but none quite matches the gaiety and splashy robustness of a tray of bulbs in full flower. In their ability to leap over the season, they give the impression that the gardener, too, can overcome the icy shackles of winter.

My winter garden grows on the swollen sill of a bay window. An assortment of plants—clivias, euphorbias, ferns, geraniums, rosemaries, and the like—surround and support various pots of bulbs. The bulbs are in differing stages of growth. Some of the crocuses show nothing more than the stubble of new grass above the soil; there are tulips whose leaves have unfurled and begun to flop like the ears of a good-natured but unloved mutt. The flower stalks of amaryllises tower above the surrounding plants, their enormous trumpets dazzling, their spines slightly stooped in the posture of all tall creatures. Scattered about this minuscule hothouse border stand large and small pots of 'Paper-White' narcissi. Their small cloud heads of white flower clusters float among the other taller plants, sometimes rising into the clear. Their fragrance floats as well; one encounters it like the perfumes of so many early spring plants—daphnes, lilacs, *Viburnum carlesii*—unexpectedly and not always in the same place. This is more true outdoors. Even in the tight quarters of our house, however, the fragrance of the 'Paper-White' shifts about, sometimes greeting you as you come through the front door, sometimes catching you from behind as you go into the kitchen, other times grabbing you as you reach the landing on the second floor.

As the flowers fade from paper white to crinkled ivory, the foliage, which is floppy from the start, begins to collapse. You can truss the leaves with metal hoops or bamboo sticks, or even bits of branch from a berried shrub, such as deciduous holly or a cotoneaster. Still, the leaves grow lanky and go weak in the knees the way all narcissus do. In a warm climate this might be the time to plant bulbs outside and let them gather their strength; here there is nothing to be done but to toss them on the compost pile. I pull the clumps out of their pots by their ears. They usually come easily with one tug because the once individual bulbs are now woven together at their roots, which have circled the pot and formed a dense web. Despite their dirty surroundings, the roots are a translucent white, and I feel somehow cruel for throwing them out. I could chop them up, I suppose, and store them in a jar, since narcissus roots are reputed to improve "long continued griefs about ye joints" as well as provide a remedy for sunburn and for drawing out splinters. But I don't grow these or other bulbs for any real practical assistance for my knees or fingers. I plant them for their sense of pure optimism, which is captured in spring, stored through summer, and revealed in the depths of winter. They seem to flower out of a blind and buoyant faith in the future. That's the kind of flower I like to have in abundance at this time of year.

MARCH

YEAR IN AND YEAR OUT SOME OF THE BEST GARDENS IN
New England come into bloom this month. March is the time
for our spring flower show, you see, and for a couple of weeks
the world is wonderfully out of kilter. The plants actually have
been off balance for some time now, tricked by the growers into
believing that spring has arrived early; and by a sleight of hand
involving bucket-loaders and bark mulch, thousands of people
enjoy the illusion that gardens grow on concrete. It will be
some time before either the plant or the show-goers do any real
growing—the plants head off to regain their strength, the gardeners go off to watch their seedlings and wait out the end of
mud season. But for the gardeners at least it is an inspiring
interlude.

Our local show combines the talents of three groups: professionals, amateurs, and a rather ill-defined assembly of tradespeople, set off in an area of their own, where you can buy most anything from a prize orchid to a personality test. Leaving this group alone for the moment, it must be said of the amateur exhibitors that they are amateurs only in the eyes of the tax collector. From single spider plants in the amateur-horticulture exhibit (open to all comers) to the carefully crafted vignettes of the various garden clubs, the efforts of these people gleam with an enviable polish that is the product of long and patient experience. In their modest size and scope the amateur exhibits lend the show a feeling of familiarity to home gardeners.

The commercial exhibits take away your breath. Large pools of people eddy around them, captivated by the wizardry of Heimlich Nursery's eighteen-foot-tall waterfall or the bounty of an enormous orchid arrangement by DeRosa's. People make notes in their programs about the new rhododendrons on display from Weston Nurseries or the rare hosta collection of Allen Haskell. The show covers just over three acres, not much by the Chelsea Flower Show's standards, but nonetheless plenty. You get a headache seeing too many good gardens all at once. Especially in March.

After the exhibits, the trade section can be a shock, but don't be put off. Alongside the folks offering to engrave your jewelry you might find the wheelbarrow you've been looking for. Perhaps a friend, still dizzy with the sight of so many tulips and the scent of lilies, will buy you a window greenhouse.

If you go, dress as you would to visit a garden in spring.

Waterproof footwear is a must; someone's pool is almost certain to spring a leak. Take a coat but be prepared to take it off. When thousands of excitable gardeners fill a single building the temperature is bound to soar.

While I wouldn't take a camera, I'm tempted to carry a small tape recorder. The commentary of so many people can be worth the price of admission. It makes for a longer stay, but it's enjoyable, sometimes even educational, silently comparing notes with fellow gardeners as they discuss the exhibits.

Short of taking a trip to England, it's hard to imagine a way of seeing so many fine gardens in such a small area, particularly in the month of March.

The education of a gardener is not a process that fits easily into a classroom, nor can it be ferreted out of books during the falls and winters of four short years. It takes as many years as you have to give, and then some. The reason, of course, is that formal knowledge is only one small ingredient of what is a complex concoction. Good gardeners, like their gardens, are distilled from a slow brew of long experience and personal alchemy. Russell Page exemplified this magical mixture, and his death on January 4, 1985, meant the loss of one of this century's great gardeners.

In his seventy-eight years Page created a dazzling array of gardens of all shapes and sizes, in locations throughout the world. He designed private gardens for all manner of royal and rich people and landscaped such notable locations as Les Halles and the Longchamps race course in Paris and the Battersea Festival Gardens in London. When he died he was deep into the development of a 145-acre park and sculpture garden at the PepsiCo world headquarters outside New York City. Page worked on small projects as well, but no matter what the sizes his designs were done for clients with means—ravines were altered, bridges demolished or built as the design demanded, waterways constructed.

Yet despite all the trappings of wealth, it is not hard to uncover the elements that distinguished Page as a great gardener and a great garden designer: his knowledge and love of plants, all of them (he maintained there was no such thing as an ugly plant), and his respect for the fundamental and practical elements of design. "I like gardens with good bones," he wrote, "and an affirmed underlying structure. I like well-made and well-marked paths, well-built walls, well-defined changes in level."

Page never owned a garden after age sixteen (his work allowed him no time for one), but through the years he was planning a special one. Perhaps more than any design he actually completed, this garden that he kept in his head and described only in the last chapter of his book, *The Education of a Gardener*, is the best example of his work. This imagined garden, he begins, "will be a small garden and a simple one." He goes on to detail the arrangements of plants, noting the particular cultivars, their relationship to the house, the nearby woods, and the stream he would include. "The mood I seek above all is one of relaxation given by a garden, easy and untortured, in which plants, however rare and strange, will grow and take their place naturally and discreetly."

That is the essential Russell Page, I think, a gardener who knew that even the simplest plot offers endless possibilities and that style in a garden is gained by constant and careful study of the site. He makes it sound simple, and his gardens make it look simple, as it should be. He never studied garden design in a formal manner; he considered himself a "garden-maker," not a teacher. But his gardens and his writing about them may still be the closest thing to a textbook we will have for some time to come.

Mention dirt to a gardener and he will answer you with a blank look. No such word exists in the vocabulary of horticulture. Check an encyclopedia on the subject and you will find no mention of the term. Donald Wyman, a man of discrimination, skips confidently from *Dirca palustris* to *Disanthus cercidifolius* in his gardening encyclopedia.

About soil there is much written (eight and a half pages by Mr. Wyman) and no doubt more spoken. Everyone agrees there are three basic types of soil—sandy, clay, and loam. But making good garden soil is not a simple matter of combining the right proportions of these three ingredients. Building up soil is a matter of feel and smell and sight. A gardener tending the soil looks nothing like a lab technician for Dow Chemical; he is closer kin to a magician bent over a hat or a witch at a cauldron, for they are in the business of producing miracles from the most ordinary components.

A gardener will jump at the chance to talk about his soil. The ritual of inspecting someone's soil involves admiring its dark-brown color, smelling the rich aroma, and testing the crumbly texture of a handful. Your host, meanwhile, will explain the ordeal of this creation you are squeezing. He will begin by telling you the state of the soil when he started—subsoil the consistency of cement. He will continue with an account of how he double-dug the place by hand, laced it with fireplace ashes, and yearly added cow manure from the one remaining farmer in the area (whom he might introduce you to, he hints). You will hear the tale of his compost pile.

The task of turning hardpan into fluffy humus is never complete. One year a gardener will turn under sharp sand and compost here to improve the drainage; the next spring you'll find him in some other part of the yard unloading a box of earthworms to tunnel through the ground, allowing air and water to reach plants' roots. In the fall there are cover crops to be planted; in the spring last fall's leaves—now composted—can be doled out to needy areas. Through the summer the gardener blankets the surface of the ground with a mulch that moderates the soil's temperature and preserves its moisture. He religiously rotates the crops, and on occasion he sprinkles trace elements over the ground.

My father pays little attention to trace elements but puts great store in the beneficial effects of manure. Every year or so he contracts for a load of manure from Austin Rumney. When he feels particularly flush he has Austin load his spreader to the brim and spread a layer over the back lawn. The manure sinks into the ground by the time the lawn is ready to mow, and the lawn in turn bristles with new growth. The gardens respond with similar vigor.

My garden is not as old as his, my soil not as mature. When we arrived, my wife and I turned up an assortment of toys left by past children, stray bones buried by dogs against lean days to come. The soil was sandy in some spots, thick clay in others. It was thin and tired throughout. We removed the bones and bricks and stray artifacts and added manure and compost and sand. You don't need to dig down far in places to find clay as hard as cement. But the color is gradually turning to a dark brown, the texture is improving, and I'm about ready to talk soil with some of my friends.

Pruning calls out the fortitude and foresight of a gardener. It is an essential task that contradicts the inclinations of any plant-loving person. Countless houses shrouded by gargantuan yews, hemlocks, and rhododendrons are sad proof of this fear of pruning. What is probably needed is a pruners' hot line that gardeners contemplating a thicket of forsythia could call for counsel and support.

Simply having the courage to prune is not enough. Pruning without a plan is as bad as not pruning at all. When we moved to our house we inherited a garden tended by a man who had no qualms about pruning. With the gusto and delicacy of a homespun barber he had squared off a hedge of forsythias, a cluster of spireas, and some young lilacs. For good measure he took a few feet off all the canes of two climbing roses and cut a couple of honeysuckles back to the ground. Then, apparently having satisfied his urge to prune, he sold the place to us and moved into a condominium.

I don't prune with such abandon, though the results sometimes give the impression of brutal treatment. Shortly after we arrived, I cut back two yews planted on either side of our front steps. They had been let to grow out of all proportion to their site and threatened to seal off the door. I cut these shaggy blobs back by half, leaving bare and scrawny skeletons to greet visitors. New growth broke from the trunks immediately, though, and by summer's end the plants looked vigorous, if not yet lush and dense.

Most of my pruning, however, is less drastic, nothing more than the regular rejuvenation and restraint of plants. Even with these jobs the decisions are never simple. The rampant-growing mock orange needs its old, punky trunks thinned out—along with a selection of the abundant new whips—but not so much that we lose the leafy curtain they provide between our property and the neighbors'. A pair of spireas want pruning that enhances the informal arch of their branches yet keeps them from flattening the bed of Japanese iris at their feet every time a rain weighs them down. With every year's pruning of the front growth, the shrubs in a sense are moved back slightly, and since we keep only strong branches, the flower-laden limbs can withstand most any weather.

The annual round of pruning also means the settling of various boundary disputes. The neighbor's wayward grapevine must be kept back from the crab apple; the English ivy is encouraged to grow along the fence but not into the lawn or onto the yakushimanum rhododendrons, which are not yet old enough to fend for themselves. Other rhododendrons have grown gangly and must themselves be kept in bounds.

There is plenty of pruning to do even in the smallest place, if the plants and the garden are to be kept healthy and happy. Although I know you should prune spring-flowering plants in summer and summer-flowering plants thereafter, I am more likely to follow Christopher Lloyd's advice that you should prune when you find the time, and early spring is usually a good time for me. The seed and plant orders are long sent but not yet received. You can't count on the weather enough to be working in the soil. But you can work outside without gloves most days, and there is a great urge to do something. Likely as not, at this time of year you can find me outside with my shears, debating the merits of some cuts.

One of the best and most obvious ways to gain more room in a garden of limited space is to grow plants that make most of their display in the air. My garden offers ample opportunities to explore this realm. There are trees and shrubs whose season is short and whose limbs are strong. There is a long, unattractive expanse of fence that wants covering. There is a south-facing garage whose stucco calls for some clothing, perhaps an espaliered magnolia. The range of plants available for this sort of gardening is increasing dramatically, and I have devoted an entire page of my spring plant list to this group.

In addition to making my choices, I have spent considerable time surveying potential planting sites. I have also made a start on getting the garden ready. My first task was to heavily prune a badly overgrown crab apple. This involved taking out one main trunk plus a number of large upper limbs. The trunk came down so easily that I decided to tackle the limb work then and there. So up into the limbs I climbed, with visions of a rambling rose giving this otherwise mundane tree a new season of beauty. I wasn't far up into the tree or long into my dreams when my feet slipped from their thin perch, sending me immediately toward the ground and into the crotch of the tree. My pants shredded and my leg gouged, I halted for the weekend my work on the vertical garden.

The next weekend found me sensibly armed with a ladder. The work went according to plan; the solid footing allowed me plenty of time to debate the merits of rambling roses ('New Dawn' vs. 'Aloha') or possibly a climbing hydrangea. No matter what I eventually plant there, the tree looks better for the preparations, and I am wiser about tree climbing.

I next turned my attentions to an established wisteria that was threatening our house and a nearby chokecherry. The wisteria is young—five or six years old, I'd guess. But in that time it had clambered over and throughout a modest trellis the previous owner had set in its path. Beyond the trellis, the vine had pried its way into an adjoining porch, around the gutters, in under the leaves of the porch. From there it had bridged the gap to the unsuspecting tree, whose limbs it girdled. Taking the better part of an afternoon, I trimmed the vine back to the confines of the trellis, although repairs to the gutter and the porch screens will need some more time.

Gardening in this vertical realm is a wonderful activity, allowing one to grow more plants in a small space, to extend and expand the season of bloom, and to surprise friends who are not used to seeing a crab apple covered with roses or a lilac studded with the blooms of a clematis. Although the fruits of such plantings are yet to come, they will be much sweeter reward for the labors and lessons of this winter.

With winter sitting stubbornly upon the garden and events elsewhere in the world swirling topsy-turvy, the future appears unsettled, and I am thankful for the steadying influence of the nursery catalogs. Their pages are rich with reports on the enduring concerns of gardeners: the weather, the land, plants, gardens, and other gardeners. Mixed in with the expected introduction to new plants, you're apt to come across commentary on the issues, large and small, that affect a nurseryman's life.

There is always plenty of activity around a nursery beyond the job of growing plants, and the owners are more than likely to write about these goings-on. In this year's edition of the Canyon Creek catalog, John and Susan Whittlesey report that they have finally finished building their new house, the progress of which you might have followed in past catalogs. In the catalog of Montrose Nursery (sadly now defunct), Nancy Goodwin gives an account of new plans accomplished in the past year, the sort of undertaking to quicken the pulse and warm the heart of any gardener:

> The new lathe house called for substantial changes in the orientation of the garden, so we removed the nearby lawn and a rose bed and put in a wide gravel path leading through the orange/purple border. There are verbenas spilling onto it and the brilliant late summer and fall display has now turned to a quiet one of grasses with graceful plumes bent by the wind. . . .

The beleaguered state of the environment is a common topic in this crop of catalogs. The matter of bulbs collected in the wild is on everyone's mind, and many companies no longer list certain bulbs because they can't be sure whether those bulbs were the products of a proper upbringing or were simply stolen from some mountainside. More and more growers make mention of the chemicals they do and don't use to grow their plants. And for packaging, numerous nurseries no longer use plastic peanuts—those white nuggets of Styrofoam that sail on the slightest whiff of wind to hide in out-of-the-way parts of the garden. In some cases the peanuts have been replaced by old newspaper or wood excelsior. Other companies now recycle peanuts, using slightly tarnished pellets presumably picked from beneath the branches of a viburnum or the cover of a mugo pine.

Coursing through the serious discussions of pesticides and plastic pellets and the excited profiles of plants is a deep vein of good humor. Allen Bush of Holbrook Nursery sets forth the details of the *Patrinia scabiosifolia* Sweepstakes, his attempt to find an appealing name for this attractive plant; the list of prizes is long and not to be believed. In the Phillip Curtis Farms catalog, Ron Menke and Carl Moseley offer their own version of the standard text about prices and terms. "The prices in this catalog . . . are subject to change without notice. (We don't intend, of course, to go around changing prices willy-nilly, but better safe than sorry.)"

For all their color printing and computer mailings, the nursery owners remain true to their heritage as growers of plants. While they are good and modern businesspeople, they seem most interested in keeping smiles on their faces. They pay attention to the people they work with and those they service, and they tend the ground out back with the care of long-term residents. As much as the ever-changing array of plants, their catalogs send a free dose of optimism, a sense of perspective, with hope for the coming spring and seasons beyond.

This is a shifting, unpredictable time of the year in our garden, when there is no telling what, if anything, will be in bloom. If the weather is settled and sunny, you may find early bulbs and shrubs tossing off their winter wraps and putting on a gay and colorful show. On the other hand, you may not even find the garden. It may have disappeared. There are, however, gardens whose season is certain. They are unaffected by the weather, neither held back by the winter's frost nor pushed ahead by the warm winds of spring. These are the flower show gardens. Theirs is the season of the imagination, and their creators are conjurers of the first order. Their peak of bloom commences in February and continues until May, with sporadic blooms throughout the other months of the year. During the height of their season, these horticultural free-for-alls fill vast warehouses, piers, and convention centers with exotic landscapes, flowers in great variety, and a heady fragrance that is part azalea, part bark mulch, part cotton candy.

The style of flower shows differs from city to city. Here in Boston, the shows generally celebrate the color and promise of spring's return to New England, with masses of narcissi, tulips, rhododendrons, azaleas, and dogwoods. Picket fences and stone walls, clapboarded buildings and brick walks set the stage. In San Francisco, home of the recently created Landscape Garden Show, the plants more often come from Australia, the Mediterranean, and the plentiful habitats of California itself. Elaborate terraces and abundant seating reflect an outdoor life that flourishes throughout the year.

Every show has a theme conceived to inspire exhibit designers. One year it might be "Gardens around the World," the next "Through the Garden Gate." In San Francisco, the theme last year was "Monopoly"; this year it is "California Heritage." Some exhibitors have their own ideas and give little heed to these themes. They devote their creative energies to figuring out a title for their exhibit that will relate to the theme while still allowing them to feature their favorite plants. Others are slavish in pursuit of the theme, and if it is "The Romantic Garden," for example, they will spare no effort in re-creating the bridge over Monet's pond at Giverny. While the themes generally have an exotic flavor, the committees that choose them should not overlook the potential of other, more modest themes. One can imagine, for example, a show devoted to "Gardens of the Gas Station and the Median Strip," or "Whirligigs and Gnomes around the World."

The larger flower shows blend the excitement of the big top with the drama of Broadway. But there is also horticultural magic at work. It takes great sorcery to rouse a cherry tree or pink dogwood into bloom in March when its natural inclination is to sleep a few more months. All praise to the men and women who can coax a delphinium into bloom—and not just one plant but ten or twenty, all topped with perfectly dense blossoms—when the ground outside is rock solid. The growers have been practicing their craft alone in greenhouses; who can blame them for adding a touch of dazzle to celebrate their accomplishments? Horticulture is the art and science of growing plants, and the wizardry of the flower shows involves plenty of both.

About this time of year there are stretches of weather—days of bright sun and warm winds—that make you want to grab your gloves and trowel and march outside. After a winter bivouacked by the fireplace with the year's collection of catalogs, these encouraging breezes bring a strong desire to take action. But now is not the time to turn over the vegetable garden or begin excavations for a new border; not when the ground is still sodden and the night is likely to bring a hard frost. If the mulch is pulled back from the beds too soon or the tiller is driven across the vegetable garden, plants or soil tilth or some such critical piece of the garden can be lost. If the gardener is not careful, if he or she cannot find suitable diversions, then the garden will be at peril.

Pruning is one alternative. There is always a certain amount of pruning that needs doing around any place. In one corner of our garden stands a young Norway maple that I go to at this time of year like a cat to a scratching post. This tree has been pruned annually for a number of years and in retaliation has suckered vigorously from every pore. I cut it back to the stumpy fists of the old shoots. This pollarding does not make an attractive tree, but it slows the growth, and come summer its scrawny looks are hidden by the foliage of other trees. Now is also the time when I make the first of the year's numerous efforts to train our wisteria. I prune in part to encourage blossoms. But just as important is the effect to discourage this plant from dismantling our porch with one arm and strangling a neighboring chokecherry with another. Then there are always the roses. Pruning them is sufficiently slow and painful enough to dampen the eagerness of any gardener for a few days.

The toolshed also presents opportunities for good deeds and distractions. All the tool handles need tending: rubbed with linseed oil, the dull wood takes on a lustrous, ruddy color and gives off a slight but sharp aroma that hints of sunshine. The shelves of pots, with their crusty, stained faces, need attention too. On a warm and promising day I am always tempted to take them out onto the lawn for a cleaning. I end up soaked, with my fingers red and raw and my mind firm about not doing this job next year until April.

Assuming the frost is out of the ground, this is a good time to drive any wobbly posts or poles back in. When I'm on this patrol, I keep a ball of twine in my coat pocket, because the pieces of string holding up clematis or roses or honeysuckles will need replacing before they are snapped by spring's vigorous new growth. The upheavals of winter's freezing will have loosened some stones and edgers as well, and these must be reset. Although I have never liked or succeeded at jigsaw puzzles, securing the underpinnings of the garden gives me the sense that I greet the spring on a firm footing.

There is compost still to spread and I usually find a clump or two of some perennial that I neglected to clean up before winter arrived. I can always sharpen the shears again, and make a scouting trip to a nursery or two. In the meantime, the season will turn to spring for good, and before long there will be more jobs than there is daylight to accomplish them. Until then I am hard at work, pottering around and marking time.

APRIL

KEEPING TRACK OF THE SEASONS AT THIS TIME OF YEAR can put a person in a spin. April is one of those months that has four weeks but easily seven or eight personalities. You wake up one Saturday morning, say, and find the sun high and warm. The birds are in the trees, catching up on gossip and testing out their wheels, and before you've done much work you break into a sweat and pull off your coat. Immediately a cloud blows in from nowhere, the day turns from blue to gray, and a chill descends. April is just that way: part June, part February.

No matter what its mood, I know when I'm in the month of April, for it marks the point when I fall seriously behind in the garden. This year was a fine case. Back in January I started drawing up plans for the coming summer. I drew from memory, and, as you know, January is no time to trust your memory about the outdoors. The yard I envisioned was twice as large as the real one, with a house half the size. I misplaced the walk and forgot most of the shrubs. When I finally got a proper plan of the yard, I began filling in the blanks. More roses, new peonies, an island bed off the back porch, some lilacs, a double-file viburnum, a patch of rhododendrons, a few extra daylilies, some hostas here and there. One or two climbing roses with complementary clematis.

I hatched these plans in January and brooded on them through February, which turned slowly into March. By the time I finished my plans (a matter of moving some plants to allow room for the volleyball tournaments I had advertised among my friends), I was running late with some of my mail orders; the companies, in return, were running low on certain plants I wanted. So I drove out to a favorite nursery (a trip of some distance) and stuffed the car with plants. Almost as soon as I got everything home and organized, Mother Nature had a nervous breakdown and let loose with a torrential rain. A number of plants died straightaway; many that didn't should have, for they never looked like anything more than survivors. I had little time to worry about them, though, for suddenly other jobs began to call out for attention: shrubs and trees to prune, firewood to move, weeding, painting—all the old duties and little time left for new vistas. It never seems like an ideal arrangement, but then that's how life goes around here in April, a month that's just as likely to give you snow as dandelions.

Early in the month of April I take the covers off the garden. Sometimes I cheat a little and start the process in March, on one of those promising days that have you thinking spring has lost its mind and returned early. Out I go to clear away the mulch in a few spots and find the nubs of early bulbs nosing their way out of the ground. Come April, I pull off the mulch in earnest.

This pulling back of mulch is not a huge job. For the most part it involves clearing away the leaves that came to rest in the beds on their own and those that were rounded up and dumped around plants of doubtful constitution. The taking off is a simple and painless task so long as I keep an eye out for plant labels and the fragile shoots of emerging plants. But there is no easy or quick way to get leaves out of the clutches of a potentilla or a spirea, or worse yet a spiny dwarf barberry or a prickly juniper.

Beneath the thin skin of boughs, branches, and leaves, the world is alive. Glistening earthworms slide out of sight as quickly as I uncover them. Along with the worms, there are of course the plants, fragile and fresh and full of promise. Many are surprises, forgotten despite the struggle to plant them. I scratch back a section of mulch and it hangs upon something. I scuffle at it with my hands and discover, oh yes, that *Chrysanthemum* 'Mary Stoker' I stuck in at the end of the season.

Most of the plants are old friends, seen in a new light. The lady's mantle no longer wears the tatty, dull-green leaves of summer's end. Now the leaves are perfect little fans, crisp and bright green. The calaminthas, thymes, and artemisias give off a faint fragrance that causes me to hunt for their small dusky foliage, barely noticeable against the soil.

At this time of year the sod is always wet and never warm. My nails, white with a winter's worth of cleaning, are immediately outlined with soil; creases on my fingers that go unnoticed in winter are stained black again. The damp soil cakes on. But the grass is soaked with dew and a few swipes cleans my hands, leaving a dark smear on the perfect green of the lawn.

Before the month's end, most of the new plants I ordered will arrive, inauspicious packages waiting on the front porch. Sent for in January and February, they too are often surprises. I unpack them immediately and assemble them on the walk out back. In the early morning I begin planting, pausing to warm my hands on a mug of coffee. The sun is not far above the horizon, and I cannot work long before the cold numbs my fingers. To plants struggling in a wrap of excelsior or newsprint, the soil is bliss. It is almost possible to feel the life come back into the limp and haggard roots as I nestle them into a planting hole. Though stiff and long dormant, my fingers also feel in the chill of the soil a dull but invigorating tingle of renewal.

Some men pass their idle hours dreaming of a den where they could go and sink into a leather chair and admire their collection of sporting trophies or stuffed animals or the photographs of them shaking hands with the president. The room I dream of would have a seat and even some shelves. But the seat would be a stool and the shelves would hold pruning shears, rolls of twine, hose attachments, and garden notebooks. What I dream about is a proper potting shed.

My present potting shed is a small room tacked onto the side of our garage. The room lacks water or electricity but is in other respects serviceable. It has a cement floor and two sets of aging metal shelves. It doesn't have a workbench, but there are countless nails in the walls and rafters for hanging watering cans, hoses, and hats. When we arrived, the room conatined rolls of chicken wire, an assortment of bamboo stakes, and two abandoned toilets. Ivy was growing on the walls, having pried its way under the decrepit window frame. The grimy window panes and the tendrils of now-withered ivy still clinging to the wall provide a suitable frame for muddy spades and trowels, hedge clippers and pruning shears.

The room I have in mind would never show up in the pages of *Architectural Digest*, for it would be plain and sturdy in the extreme, like the old laundry rooms with their enormous soap-stone sinks and drying racks that used to exist in the basements of substantial homes. My plans call for two large sinks (for washing plants and pots as well as to have a place for spilling things generally). Shelves would climb the walls, holding everything from pots in all sizes to labels, boxes of nails, balls of twine, and stray coffee mugs (for such a room would be a nice place to start out chilly mornings). Tools of all rank would hang in orderly fashion on a wall or two, though I wouldn't want a penciled outline of each to signify its place. Bags and bins of soils and fertilizers would sit under the benches; baskets, wet gloves, and drying flowers and vegetables could hang from the rafters. The layout would allow a wheelbarrow to come and go, but lawn mowers would be forbidden. That's what garages are for. Finally, and perhaps most important, there would have to be windows looking out to the garden. Such a room is a place in which to gather not only supplies and equipment but also ideas and dreams.

A potting area is the nerve center of any garden, no matter its size, and every gardener finds a place and a way to make such a place. Few gardeners enjoy luxurious work areas. Potting sheds are usually rooms left over in buildings once used for something else: an abandoned structure like a barn, say, or a garage. One friend makes use of an old chicken shack. Some people simply annex space in the garage or the cellar, or even in the kitchen, setting aside metal pots for clay ones and giving pride of place under the sink to bags of potting soil. This is a perfectly fine way of doing things; many plants are raised and cared for in this manner. As with a garden, it's not the size or location of a potting shed that matters. In both cases what counts is that there is ample room for improvements in the future.

At this time of year you have only to turn your back and a glorious spring day, sunny and in the sixties, will turn into an arctic evening. Instead of dreaming about the coming splendors of your garden, you are up at midnight, clad in your pajamas and a pair of clammy boots, draping an assortment of old shirts and perfectly good sheets over emerging plants that also got taken in by a stretch of balmy days. This year we will be watching the nights with particular attention, as it has already been a trying winter for plants, many of which spent a long spell buried beneath snow and ice and, in the case of one dwarf potentilla, beneath snow and a large brown garbage can, which was misplaced.

All sorts of bulbs are making their annual progress here and there around the yard. In one part of the lawn a circle of snow-drops marks the site where a hydrangea used to be. I dug it out last fall in the hope of letting more sunlight into a shady cor-ner of our garden. A climbing rose ('New Dawn') that runs up the southern side of our front door is showing thick and pointed leaf buds along the length of its stems. In the peren-nial bed bits and pieces of plants pry their way up into the mulch; shortly everything except for late risers such as Japanese anemones and hostas will be visible. Still, that is no reason to believe spring has arrived.

Although it's too early to do any digging or gardening of that sort, I have lots of pruning to keep me busy and a new set of pruning shears to help with the work. After a couple years of failing health my old pruners died at the end of last summer. It was just as well, since they wouldn't stay closed and I had ripped a number of pants pockets by forgetting their habit of springing open at any moment. The new pruners are sturdier and more comfortable. If I can remember that they will not double as a saw, this set should last for many years.

Even at this early date I am behind on the pruning in our garden. The problem is not that I dislike the job or am especially lazy about it but that I never know what to do with all the trimmings once I've finished. Some clippings I use to prop up short, floppy plants. I use the sturdier branches to stake campanulas and surround peonies—that sort of thing. All the same, the leftovers exceed my needs. So put them on the compost pile, you say. Unfortunately the compost pile, like the garden, is a small one—a very small one. I suppose I could shred all the bits of spirea and mock orange and lilac, but that is a slow and noisy process and to my mind not worth the reward. Otherwise, I am left to tie the pieces up into small bundles for the trash collectors. This doesn't seem right somehow, and so I end up putting off the pruning longer than I should. I probably would have waited even longer if it weren't for the new shears that need breaking in.

I enjoy pruning at this time of year; it's an activity best done slowly and with deliberation, just the pace for a gardener coming out of hibernation. I may take a couple days just getting things right with our spireas. There is no rush. Spring is in the air, to be sure, but not yet in the ground.

There is something in the spirit of the early-spring flowers that appeals to gardeners. Perhaps it's their foolhardy determination, the way they have of dragging out their summer hats and sunglasses at the slightest suggestion of spring, while anyone with any sense sits inside bundled in sweaters. Not the crocus or the adonis. Not the snowdrop. Show them a few sunny days, pass a warm breeze over their heads, and they break into full bloom. Like the gardeners who tend them, the spring flowers risk everything to get outdoors again.

The forsythia shares the early-season fever of these other plants. A drab and derelict character for all but a few weeks of the year, it redeems itself in the earliest spring with golden-yellow flowers that are radiant against the brown and gray backdrop of the late-winter landscape. Well tended, a forsythia in bloom is a fountain of yellow, its long branches arching gracefully away from the plant. Most often the plant is not so well tended, not so graceful a sight, being either an unruly tangle or an over-pruned globe.

Last fall my wife and I spent the better part of two weekends wrestling seven bedraggled forsythias from an area we wanted for other shrubs. I knew the common complaints leveled against the plant: its gaudy flowers, boring foliage, and gangly habit. I understood that a gardener of good opinion must banish them from sight. With some effort that is what we finally did.

However, as you might guess, with the arrival of spring I find myself missing them. True, they were too many and too large for the spot they claimed as their home. But maybe there is room enough for one of the smaller cultivars, such as 'Arnold's Dwarf', which grows only two or three feet tall. I might also plant *F. suspensa* or one of its hybrids against a wall of our house, as I have seen it done, training its flexible wands to a trellis. Weston Nurseries notes that this species is good for "overwall" planting, which sounds like an interesting idea but one that must wait. In our present surroundings anything that goes over a wall ends up in our neighbor's yard, and he already has a substantial stand of forsythia.

The forsythia endures in many gardens despite disparaging words all around. In his lengthy remarks on this plant, Mr. Thomas Everett allows: "Except for grand displays of bloom, ease of cultivation, and general freedom from pests and diseases, forsythias have little to recommend them." Should we say of spring that except for following winter, being filled with magical sights, rich scents, and an air of warm contentment overall, it has little to offer? I throw my vote in with the people of Brooklyn, who claim the forsythia as their official flower. It's not a perfect plant. All the same, its somewhat unruly display remains one of spring's indomitable delights.

Spring appears on the calendar on March 20, but it doesn't show up at our place until a month or more later. I suspect that earlier date is only the day when spring leaves South Carolina, or wherever it was playing golf, and heads north for the season. I judge its arrival in large part by the appearance of the first packages from the mail-order nurseries. The boxes are plain and in many cases recycled. (At first glance it appears you've received a shipment from an electrical supplies firm in Knoxville, Tennessee.) To the uninitiated, the contents are nothing but spindly sticks, grizzled root balls, tiny pots sporting minute clumps of foliage. To a gardener, however, these are the makings of roses and magnolias and herbaceous borders. In many ways they embody the spirit of spring. From their leafless, half-dead beginnings will come the flowers of summer and the bones of borders to come. All that, hidden in a brown box stuffed with old newsprint, is enough to make anyone believe in higher powers.

Just when the shipments will appear, however, is a matter of great concern to a gardener. Most nurseries offer the option of stating your preferred shipping date. This is a tempting idea, but one fraught with peril. Settling on a date causes me nearly as much anxiety as does factoring in the postage and handling fees for an order. You need to pick a time that's far enough along in the season so that plants coming from gentle regions such as California and the South don't freeze in an air-freight way station in Albany, New York. On the other hand you need to get them safely to your home before the season warms up too much or they may cook in some tractor trailer along a Virginia interstate. The plan is to stagger the arrivals so that they occur gradually, but always on Thursdays or Fridays. Sadly, Nature and the Gods of Shipping do not always listen to gardeners. Do what you may, more than half of your orders will arrive all at once on a Monday or Tuesday.

Still, there is no better tonic at the end of a day, especially a Monday, than to find a package waiting for you on the front steps. Our delivery person must be a gardener, for he always tucks them under a bench on the porch, out of the sun but still visible. The days when the porch is empty are a letdown, but when a package—or better yet a stack of them—sits there, I am immediately refreshed. A packing slip with no back orders is the best sort of mail at this time of year.

Unpacking these shipments is a delicate business and not for the heavy-handed. You need a surgeon's touch for teasing fragile young stems and leaves from thickets of excelsior, newsprint, and Styrofoam peanuts. A few casualties are bound to occur, but if the roots are strong, the plants will revive. The bareroot plants I heel in the vegetable garden. The others I stand in the shade of the ginkgo out back, where they can stretch and breathe fresh air.

Once the packages begin to arrive, it is time to wake the garden, pull mulch off the borders, finish the pruning. I get up earlier and shuffle out to where the recent arrivals are clustered. Then I begin to take them around, laying them out on the lawn at the edge of the garden where I expect to plant them. These plans are apt to change. One thing is sure, however: There is no going back on the season. The packages are coming on, and it's full steam ahead into spring.

The instructions for making a lawn are simple and straightforward. You can find them in a hundred different books, repeating age-old notions about peat and lime, sowing, rolling, and sprinkling. Last spring after a crew of carpenters departed our yard we had no choice but to plant a new lawn. The old lawn was woeful enough before the builders arrived; after a fall and winter of their lumber piles and their general tromping around we were finally forced to start fresh. It seemed a small, uncomplicated task.

The activity got under way on a bright Saturday morning in

April when two men from a local rental company deposited an aging eight-horsepower rototiller on our front walk. While my wife (nearing the end of a pregnancy) and her visiting brother drove off to gather supplies, I started up the tiller, which bore the scars of a life of rental abuse. All the same, it turned over without great trouble, and we began circling the yard. It churned slowly on, hunkering down into soft soil or suddenly jumping forward where its tines tried but failed to grip an unseen boulder or a far-wandering tree root. Each time this happened, the jolt dislodged the shifting lever. I found myself lurching around the yard stooped over to hold the lever in place. Because this required the posture and gait of a hunchback, I shut down the engine and spent a half hour rigging a wire sling to hold the lever in place.

When my wife and her brother at last returned with peat moss, superphosphate, and lawn seed (they had been held up with a flat tire), we spread a three-inch layer of peat moss over the ground and tilled it in until the soil was light brown and fluffy. Unfortunately, we'd forgotten to add the superphosphate. There was no chance of using a spreader at this point; it would bog down in the soil. Furthermore, the instructions for spreading fertilizers and the like never match up with the settings on my machine, which has calibrations unlike any others. So we spread the superphosphate by hand and circled the yard with the tiller one last time.

Now, as the directions instruct, the next step is to roll the ground (with your roller half full of water, preferably). I don't own a roller; instead the three of us boot-packed the ground, marching round and round the lawn-to-be like a high-school band practicing its halftime maneuvers. This left the lawn mostly firm, although it showed none of the smooth, level grade and professional finish that a contractor would produce. With some effort we were able to haul the spreader back and forth across the lumpy ground, laying down a dense cover of seed. I then scuffed the seed lightly, worrying all the time about how light is really light. Finally, to conclude (and celebrate) the job, I gave the new seedbed a gentle soaking.

I don't know what effect all this had on my wife, but about four the next morning she woke me with the news that we were heading for the hospital. While she packed some last items, I went down and watered the new lawn, not knowing how soon I might get back to the job. The baby, a girl, arrived shortly after midday, two weeks early. The lawn appeared two weeks later, just as I was beginning to fear it might not appear at all.

It turned out to be quite a weekend, more exciting and far more complicated than the textbooks ever let on.

The nurseryman who sells plants through the mail maintains strange relations with the seasons. On the one hand he is a farmer like any other, his year an ongoing cycle of planting in spring, harvesting in fall. But he is also part postman, and by the time the farmer part of him gets going on his spring jobs, the postman part is six months off, working on fall. Just when he hits a lull in the farming and thinks about taking a break, he finds the mail room filling up with orders. It's satisfying work, but the vacations don't come often or last long.

Most mail-order nurseries now handle all their orders with the help of a computer or two, so the days of friendly correspondence have for the most part disappeared and been replaced by anonymous forms. Happily, certain other old customs still exist that give some idea of the personalities of the proprietors and the lives they're living. A few of the firms are small enough to recognize my name as a regular customer, and every few seasons an extra plant will arrive with an order. There is no note—holding down two jobs, even on a small scale, doesn't leave much time for writing—but the plant choice lets me know that the owner remembers the sort of plant I've ordered in the past and has opinions of his own about what I need.

A number of the companies I order from still wrap their plants or stuff their boxes with local newspapers. This is a good chance to find out what sort of place your nurseryman is living in. Generally there's lots of local school sports and regional politics. The advertising sections don't offer much, but the police notes can make good reading. All in all it's an invigorating reminder of how big this country is and how many concerns are common to us all.

One of the side effects of the computers is that gardeners end up receiving multiple copies of most catalogs. This situation can't be blamed on the nurserymen, at least in my case, for I have been throwing them curveballs. The problem starts slowly: You order twice in one year, the first time claiming yourself as Jon White and the next time, in a more formal mood, as Mr. Jonathan L. White. A nearsighted computer fails to notice your erratic ways and sends you two copies of the next catalog. One copy you take with you on the bus to work, and one you leave at home. In both you mark plants you need (or at least want). Before you remember there are two lists you send off your first order; then you mail off the second. Finally, you decide to pick up one last plant, and feeling foolish for having already sent two orders, you send this one off in your wife's name. Come next season you will receive yet a third catalog. You may receive a good many more if your wife has also been passing herself off as two or three different people. There is really no telling where this chain reaction might end.

It's no doubt disorienting for the nurseryman, but for the gardener the mail-order business has a lot to recommend itself. It's possible to find most any plant you want (or any seed, for that matter). It's an agreeable pastime hunting for plants, and you invariably find new prospects along the way. The task of drawing up orders and thinning them out can be a sustaining activity in the dead of winter. And just when you've given up hope on spring, long after you've forgotten your orders, plain brown boxes begin appearing at your door. It may be the end of winter for you, but it's the height of spring for a nurseryman.

In one corner of our basement sits a mound of sheets and shirts and pillowcases. It is a ragtag collection; the sheets are all different colors and worn through in places. The shirts are beyond

74

repair, their pockets torn, their collars frayed. A number no longer have arms. If I enjoyed repairing cars I would tear them all into small squares and give myself a lifelong supply of rags. But I have ceased my efforts at engine repair and spend my spare time trying to keep our garden running. These weary sheets and shirts constitute our defense against late frosts. We are protecting not only the results of our own optimism—those seeds and seedlings we've set out—but also the enthusiasm of the established plants, many of which have already shouldered their way out of the ground and sit prey to sudden, chilling frosts that slip down from Canada overnight.

Once the season starts in earnest and plants are showing clearly, I keep a special eye on the weather reports. It may just be my nervous system, but I get jumpy any time the forecaster cheerfully warns of frost overnight. I should know better than to believe a forecaster. He is interested in making the weather sound like news and doesn't worry that in doing so he condemns scores of gardeners to useless labor and fitful sleep. But you can count on me to haul the shirts and sheets out of the basement and drape them over as many plants as I have pieces of cloth. Often it's past midnight when my unease finally turns into full-blown panic, and so I wind up shuffling around the yard in a get-up of pajamas, boots, and jacket, with a bundle of sheets in my arms and a flashlight clenched in my teeth. Invariably I lack enough coverings to protect all the plants. So inside I go, tracking mud behind me, to rummage for a sheet that shows signs of fading.

The scene next morning must surprise our neighbors.

Scattered about the yard is a lumpy patchwork of bedraggled clothing and bedding. (One year I enlisted an old brown blanket used for protecting furniture during moves. It weighed a ton when wet, though, and began smelling strangely, so I sent it to the landfill.) After breakfast I lift the coverings. This goes quickly for the most part, although there is always a lengthy battle at the rosebushes. They do not let go without a struggle and stern words from me.

Frost is not the only thing that endangers a garden in early spring. In fact, I mostly worry not about the last frost but about other threats that come in late spring and can be far crueler than a high-pressure system from Manitoba. Count among these the painters who arrive with the express purpose of tramping back and forth across your emerging plants. On their last visit they managed (I'm not sure how) to sever a four-year-old clematis at ground level. I am also on guard against the tree crew that comes every couple of years to limb the Norway maples and let light into the garden. They never arrive in winter, when the ground is frozen; they wait until the ground is wet and soft. They stand on those plants the painters missed and drop branches on the adolescent viburnum that showed promise of flowering this year.

There are many surprises that greet the gardener in spring, many of them unrelated to weather and unaffected by old bed linens. Hardiness is often not an issue as much for the plants as for the gardener, whose nerves are vulnerable to disturbances day and night.

The catalogs may captivate a gardener in the winter with plants unknown, but come spring I put away my stack of mail-order temptations and visit the local nurseries. With the catalogs in hand I dream about the possibilities of exotics such as phormium and brugmansia, cistus and hebe. At the nursery I wander among hollies and rhododendrons, roses, and dogwoods, and covet them nonetheless. Winter without catalogs would be grim; spring without an outing to a favorite nursery would be unbearable.

This spring trek of mine is largely a ritual. Although I invariably return with something propped in the backseat, the garden no longer allows for the massive buying sprees that used to see my driving home with boxes of perennials stacked in the foot wells and the trunk, shrubs wedged into seats forward and rear. Now I go for the occasional replacement—and because, in spring, a nursery brimming with plants and scented with bark mulch and peat moss is an uplifting place.

I usually make the forty-five-minute trip on a Saturday. I start early, at 8 A.M., when the uncluttered highway encourages daydreaming about perfect gardens. The nursery lies inland, just at the fringe of the country, and is probably a zone colder than my own garden. From the trees and shrubs and front yards along the road I can check the season's progress as well as the winter's toll. Just off the turnpike there is a diner where I usually stop for breakfast, coffee at least, and a last run through the nursery's catalog. No need to rush these things.

Who can deny the attraction of rhododendrons and the like at this time of year? The congregation of a hundred or so plants greeting me at the nursery's front gate, perfectly grown and clotted with blossoms in every shade from pale white to glowing crimson, still excites me. Sometimes I wonder how I've escaped a garden of nothing but rhododendrons. With the promise that I'll pick up just one *R.* 'Molly Fordham' on the way out, I move on to the hollies and boxwoods, imagining which plant I would load into my cart. Around the corner stands a sampling of the grafter's art: weeping birch and bobbed pines. I can't tell you where they might go in my garden, but I have come close to carting one or another home some years.

. The morning passes in this way. Japanese maples, euonymus, plums, pears, apples, dogwoods, roses—I examine and admire them all, checking prices, choosing favorites, dismissing others. My last stop is the perennial beds. They are laid out across a broad, often sunny slope, each row of plants marked and identified with a thick white wooden label. Simple roofs of snow fencing protect shade lovers and recently set out plants. As with the trees and shrubs, the clumps of alyssum, bleeding heart, lungwort, and the like punctuate the otherwise green rows with their bright but delicate flowers. Thoughts of *R.* 'Molly Fordham' fade. What's needed is some phlox, perhaps, maybe some spiderwort, another hellebore. Or a Japanese silver-painted fern.

I always buy something though rarely very much. I know most of the plants by heart and could probably find my way through the place with my eyes closed. Nonetheless, I return each spring to hatch dreams and convince myself that another season is finally fully under way.

Although you cannot count on the weather in April, there are more good days than bad. We can still get a frost, of course, and there is usually some wet snow, but the temperature during the day can climb into the seventies, the soil is workable, and activity in the garden begins in earnest. The first job of the new season usually is to gather up the remains of the one gone by. I know gardeners exist who tidy their gardens thoroughly before winter; in England the truly fastidious folks prick over their borders with a fork at the end of fall, scuffling the top layer of soil slightly to leave a uniform mulch of soil for winter appearance. But I cannot imagine a spring that did not begin on hands and knees paying final tribute to the previous year.

The first order of business is to trim away the matted foliage of plants such as irises, daylilies, peonies, and hostas. All of them hold up well into the fall and turn handsome shades of yellow and bronze. But winter works on them, and by spring they are limp, stringy masses, which nonetheless hold tight to their roots. Tug as you will, you will come away with only a handful of squishy brown pulp. No, you must cut away the foliage with your shears bit by bit, as though you were cleaning burdocks from a collie. More easy to tend are the bergenias, which pretend to be evergreen but lose many of their leaves. These blackened paddles pull away from the crown easily, revealing the plant's main stalk, which is the color of a raw bruise. The muddy, moldy leaves of pulmonarias and the brittle, wasted fronds of ferns, both of which I fold over the plants' crowns in fall as a quick and easy mulch, must now be snipped away. The still-standing stalks of aconitums, lilies, sedums, and such separate with a quick twist. I cut the sturdy stubble of coreopsis, liatris, and lavender roughly with my hedge shears, making final cuts with pruning shears as needed. This work on the lavender is especially pleasing, as the weathered, lifeless stalks still hold a hint of their perfume and will stain you with their fragrant oils as a reward for your effort.

The real reward for this labor—aside from a healthier garden—is the chance to see your garden at this very early stage. Scratch aside the damp, dark brown, partially decayed leaves and you reveal the rosettes of geraniums, sedums, and heucheras, all tight bunches of perfectly crimped and glistening foliage. Elsewhere you can find the lime-green spears of lilies, irises, and pulmonarias; the ruby-colored snouts of peonies; and the tight knuckles of ferns.

As you work, your eyes regain the focus they lost with the onset of winter, and you suddenly pick out the fuzzy twigs of, say, *Coreopsis verticillata* or the rosy bristles of *Epidemium rubrum*. You will notice emerging plants that you had forgotten. Not only will you discover the plants you had planted, you will remember the plans that you made last fall. Slowly the dormant skills and instincts of gardening return, resuscitated like the plants themselves.

For all the destruction and havoc that winter heaps upon the garden, spring brings an opposite and sometimes equal burst of rejuvenation. Often the eruption of spring surpasses all the devastations that occur, and one gets the feeling that the process of entropy has overlooked the garden.

Probably the most fruitful—and least desirable—plants in my garden are the Norway and silver maples, which practice all forms of self-propagation with abandon. They seed themselves about as though the world were coming to an end. In earliest spring they stand quietly. Unsuspecting gardeners may decide that theirs don't engage in such profligate behavior. Then the seedlings begin to appear; with each day the number increases in staggering leaps and bounds. In the matter of making a family, these maples easily outpace a lovesick rabbit. If you get to the seedlings before they establish a real root, you can slip them out of the ground with a slight tug. Turn your back, however, and by fall they'll make an entrenched forest. The list of plants with such unbounded fruitfulness is long, including such gems as kudzu, Japanese honeysuckle, and *Rosa multiflora*. All of them have their defenders no doubt (as, I'm sure, do Norway and silver maples), but they have never found their way into our garden.

We do grow lots of other rampant plants. Every one offers some attraction, and they are all easily checked in their wayward ways. The dusky-leaved *Viola labradorica* scatters itself broadly and quickly. It may yet become a pest because it is small and easily overlooked, but so far I enjoy the dark smear the leaves spread across the garden floor. Hardy geraniums also run wild, springing up the width and breadth of the border.

The new seedlings seem delicate—a floppy hat of foliage wobbling above a thin strand of stem. But the root they set down is sturdy. You will have to struggle to remove it, grabbing it down around the shoulders and working it up out of the ground. Scotch thistles, on the other hand, unfurl their silver rosettes in great numbers each spring, but in the first year their long carrotlike root slides easily from the soil.

Some of the most interesting and desirable plants readily make more of themselves. Among this crowd I would put the hellebores and certain daphnes, which annually surround themselves with offspring, and *Euphorbia myrsinites*, whose snakelike seedlings coil out of the tiniest cracks in our sidewalks. Like lots of plants, they seem to know just when to place themselves. The gangly *Verbena bonariensis* shares this trait. This will also be a year of many foxgloves. The seedlings appeared last year in great patches, building strength through the summer to ready themselves for this spring. And we can count on bumper crops of verbascums and eryngiums. The salixes as a group send offshoots whenever they find a chance, as do many viburnums and caryopteris. Even stolid plants like rhododendrons will layer readily if you happen to get a little heavy-handed with the mulch.

As if this free flood of plants were not enough, plenty of others will be ready for division this spring, willing candidates for a fishes-and-loaves routine. The real question is not how to fill in all the holes left by winter losses but rather how to deal with the surplus of new plants spilling out of the garden in an encouraging display of nature's vitality.

One of the pivotal days in the gardening year is the first day of digging. This day is not noted on calendars, which is a good thing since the exact day moves around from year to year. It is a moment gardeners watch for; in this part of the country the ground generally is warm and dry enough for digging sometime in April. The frost may be out of the ground well before then, of course, and there may be many things in flower, but the soil is still too wet for turning. So gardeners must wait anxiously until the day when the soil crumbles easily in their hands. This marks a turning point in the season, and signals the return to the garden and the chance to put long-simmering plans and schemes into action.

We don't have much opportunity or need for digging at our place. The borders are all well established. The vegetable garden is set. There is a good bit of lawn that I have my eye on, but it is reserved for lounging and soccer games. For the last couple years the amount of spadework has been diminishing, and I have been left with little to do other than replacing plants that have died or fallen out of favor and reshaping the edges of borders (and expanding them in the process). This is a good year for digging because we are taking out a hedge of barberry and replacing it with arborvitae, a project that will involve considerable digging.

The process of spading up ground is always one of discovery, for the ground is a grab bag of unexpected bounty. Turn over a shovelful of soil and it may contain anything from knives and forks, bottles and glasses, to lost college rings and discarded spark plugs. One could stock a tool chest from the gleanings of some gardens: tape measures, hammerheads, screwdrivers. Usually there are reminders of children—the pale and dirty plastic dolls, the rusted toy cars and tractors. Our ground has offered up a typical assortment of belt buckles, nails, and keys to unknown doors. After you garden in a place long enough you begin finding your own belongings: the misplaced watch or forgotten pocketknife.

The digging to create a garden usually exposes relics of gardens past as well. There are stumps and root balls of plants long dead, labels, and traces of potting mixes with their telltale specks of perlite. I have come across stumps of catalpas, lilacs, pines, and maples, all reminders of a previous owner who loved trees and planted one edge of the property with a dense assortment of specimens. They are invisible now but not forgotten in the spring spadework. When archeologists began studying the soils around Monticello, Thomas Jefferson's home, stains in the soil showed where fruit trees and other plants had once grown. Digging in our borders, coming upon the skeletons of long-gone trees, I sometimes can imagine the property when it was heavily treed, with a tall canopy casting shade across the lawn to the street.

Even without the images and artifacts of the past, I would be restless to dig in spring. There is something satisfying and fortifying about digging, a feeling that mixes the simple, childlike pleasure of stirring up the soil with the satisfaction of creation, which begins with that plunging of spade or shovel into the ground.

MAY

MAY IS A MONTH FULL OF PROMISE FOR THE GARDENER and for the garden. The garden is green and vigorous and unblemished. The gardener under the spell of May is almost equally green and vigorous and unblemished. In May he makes new promises and sets aside old ones. This year, he says, I will deadhead the rhododendrons. I will take photographs of the garden each month and keep up with my journal. Every day I'll inspect the plants for trouble. The new retaining wall will be completed this month, he tells himself, and I shall buy more pots to fill with summer-flowering bulbs for the front steps. But while he is off making good on these vows, the black aphids begin to cluster on the mock orange. (Last year he said he would watch them.) The peonies suddenly want staking, as do the delphiniums. He is only halfway done with the retaining wall, though, and can't think of stopping right now. He does find time one afternoon to treat the lawn, which looks shabby and lifeless, to a meal of fertilizer and weed killer. It doesn't occur to him that probably the lawn is simply recovering from his last outing with the spreader.

Perhaps a gardener is outside the law in springtime, but he should show some restraint around the nurseries. Throughout the winter he reminded himself that he already owned enough plants to supply the entire neighborhood, to say nothing of the many divisions he must make in the fall. Add to that the rare bergenias he had to order, the three geraniums a friend sent unannounced, and, oh yes, the Japanese anemones he saved from a neighbor's compost pile. Yet come May he drives over to the local nursery to buy a flat of annuals for the window boxes and returns home with two new clematises, three thalictrums, and a few (well, four) irises. As a present for his wife he purchases a special mountain laurel. The list of items he decided not to buy is longer by far.

May is not without troubles, to be sure. For no reason a downspout disconnects itself from its gutter, nearly drowning a clematis and a 'Betty Prior' rose. Sometime during the month a hard frost skulks in, and the gardener wakes to find his prize aconitums blackened and withered. He faces other challenges as well. The squirrels have stopped raiding the bird feeders; they are now digging for grubs in the lawn. That these excavations bespeak a healthy lawn does not comfort the gardener. He would rather have a sick lawn without the pockmarks. He is distracted by the cats, too. They have not forgotten him or his campanulas, which they enjoy hiding under large mounds of soil. Like the squirrels, these cats come in the night, and he sometimes imagines that if he turned on the floodlights at two in the morning he would find the yard filled with animals cavorting and doing their best to tear things up.

He ought to take action, and he might. Yet he is sidetracked in the morning when he goes outside and discovers that another astilbe has unfurled its rusty fronds. Elsewhere, a hosta he thought dead has proved him wrong. The geraniums from a friend show signs of life as well. It will be a fine day, he decides, indeed, a good season. So he sprinkles some seed on the torn lawn, then settles the campanula back into place and goes off to work. A gardener intoxicated with the promise of May cannot be crushed by a few mild rebukes. In May all is promise.

I come from a family of lawn makers. One way or another, I have studied and practiced the fine points of lawn making from an early age. When I was growing up this involved little more than endless mowing. We lived in Vermont, where moderate summer temperatures and ample moisture make for great turf and almost constant mowing. So I spent many hours prodding a lethargic push reel mower along the steep bankings, in under the long boughs of the fir trees, and along the edges of the stone walls. The job seemed never-ending and was made worse by my father's decision every few years to reclaim another patch of the tangle of hardhack and alders for lawn.

Somewhere along the way we acquired a Locke reel mower, a large and serious machine with two wings and a small sulky. All iron and steel and painted a dark green, it was directly descended from the early tractors and steam engines, massive creatures and all business. At top speed it moved hardly faster than a man's pace. The three sets of reels whirled furiously, however, spewing a glistening green wake that stained your sneakers and filled the cuffs of your pants.

I wasn't allowed to drive this beast for some years. Considerable strength was needed to maneuver it around the trees and other corners that fill any lawn. You drove it with finesse, timing, and the grace of God, pulling on the inside handle, depending on the direction you wanted to go, and letting the machine pivot around you the way a marching band turns, the inside marking time while the outside arcs around. Let the low rumble of the engine lull you for a moment and a wing would surely snag the base of some shrub or a clump of thick weedy grass at the lawn's edge and drag the machine off into the thicket before you could even reach the controls. For such a slow-moving machine, it raised havoc in a hurry.

When I was fifteen, I surrendered my amateur status as a lawn mower and took up with Hud Carpenter's lawn crew. Even though I considered myself a veteran, Hud confined my duties to the rotary mowers used for finish work. The big machines belonged to Claude Tarbell and his brother, Clifford. These two cared little for lawns or mowers or artistry. They did love powerful engines and drag racing, though, and took any opportunity to race their mowers around the lawns and to and from the truck. This shortened the life of Hud's machines, no doubt, but it helped to pass the summer. For my part I gained a lasting dislike of hand clippers and lost my enthusiasm for lawns for a number of years.

The lawn I tend these days is hardly big enough to turn a Locke mower around in and not big enough to warrant any sort of power mower for that matter. Partly for the sake of my ears and partly in deference to those earlier mowers, I cut this lawn with a push mower. It's a simple machine with a sixteen-inch reel and a plastic hopper that hooks behind the wheels and catches the grass. I tried the hopper for a time but gave it up. The bucket needed emptying every couple passes, and I spent most of my time hiking to and from the compost pile. So now I let the clippings fall where they may and use the hopper when I'm weeding or deadheading.

The mower is small; it inspires no fear. My old associates Claude and Clifford would scoff at it. But it rolls out the orderly stripes along the lawn, and the whirling reel still fills my cuffs with fragrant green clippings.

Following the advice of Mr. Thoreau as well as the natural inclination of most every gardener, I have been building castles in the air. I should be tending to the lawn and erecting a fence out front, but recently my time has been spent up in the air— in the trees, to be precise.

My yard is equipped with a full set of trees. They are mostly large trees, far larger than I would like, and they produce shade and squirrels in abundance. Although I plan to thin them out sometime this season, what I really would like to do is take up some timber and construct a tree house.

A tree house is considered a plaything of children, and any gardener with sense would rather construct a raised bed than a raised house. But back a few hundred years, gardeners felt otherwise. In the sixteenth and seventeenth centuries, quite a number of European gardens, particularly in Italy, included elaborate tree houses in their design. The stairway circling up into a tree was in some instances broad enough for two people to make the ascent side by side; other tree houses sported hidden fountains that could shower unsuspecting visitors. In Holland and Germany and Switzerland, gardeners often trained the branches to create walls, roofs, or floors.

I shared the tenancy of a tree house with my brother for some years when I was younger. The house, which sat about fifteen feet up in the crook of a large sugar-maple tree, had walls and a roof of plywood; its windows swung up to the ceiling in response to an elaborate pulley system. Likewise, a small table with hinged legs would swing down from the wall by means of other pulleys and rope. Readying the house for action involved a process similar to getting a marionette into motion.

A number of years after the demise of that tree house I spent some time in another much grander structure, a three-story house that began twenty feet up in an enormous elm tree and continued on up for another fifteen feet. The builders had constructed the house in such a way that the tree limbs moved freely without ripping themselves or the structure apart.

Finished neatly in weathered barnboard, the house had balconies, a bay window, and a dumbwaiter. The roof was a large deck hidden in the crown of the tree's foliage from which you had a panoramic view of the surrounding fields. It was a grand palace as tree houses go, and the view out though the leaves from a height of fifty feet made my heart beat fast in a mixture of delight and dizziness.

I have neither the skill nor the heart to attempt such a structure, but I could do with a simple platform stretched across the branches of one of the maples out back. I wouldn't even put on a roof, just a floor and a comfortable seat or two. No walls, either—they cut down on the view and the breeze, which smells sweeter up fifteen feet or so. And I'd want a spot to keep a pad of paper and some pencils for those ideas that are bound to occur when your head is up in the air.

Something attracts people to a house with roses climbing their way up the walls and maybe arching over the front door. In summer the canes thick with foliage snake across the face of the house, sparkling with sunlight and casting rich shadows. In winter the bare canes etch an elegant pattern and hint of spring's promise. Our house is a simple structure, mostly square, shingled, and with little in the way of ornament. So the roses growing on either side of the front porch are a graceful addition to the architecture, softening its hard edges with abundant clusters of vibrant flowers framed by glossy leaves. There is something exciting and romantic about these climbers—a look of lushness and luxuriance (for the canes reach to the second floor) and the suggestion that the garden, not the gardener, is in control.

The walls weren't always cloaked in roses. English ivy covered the shingles on two sides and part of a third when we arrived. It blanketed the walls—and some of the windows—a dull-green mat that hinted of suffocation rather than scintillation. I tore off the ropy, slightly bristled stems and began the process of training three roses in their stead.

The instructions you will find in books don't exactly match the roses you will find in your garden. Those canes you hope to train in a certain direction sulk all summer, while long and lethal whips surge out in all the wrong directions. There is some question about exactly what is a flowering shoot and what is not. Furthermore, the annual process of pruning is not only confusing, it's painful. You cannot properly conduct business with a climbing rose while wearing heavy gloves. Without them you cannot avoid puncturing your hands, to say nothing of the random scratches you inflict on your arms, shoulders, and head as you gingerly move about the garden trying not to hurt other plants. One year I decided simply to chuck all the clippings over my shoulder onto the lawn, where I could then gather them up for the compost pile. This would eliminate the need to move around in the garden so much and get the prunings out of my hands quickly. Unfortunately, some fell in the garden, short of the lawn, and some smaller pieces escaped the lawn rake, and that summer we pulled thorns from bare feet and fingers and plotted a new strategy.

Our first blooms appear sometime late this month, on 'New Dawn', a six-year-old plant that sits in a protected ell on the south side of our house. The longest canes are twelve feet or so; by leaning out one of the second-floor windows one can sample the flowers' gentle fragrance. A few of the canes cut across a portion of a living-room window so that in summer people sitting inside feel as though they are in a bower, surrounded by green with rose shadows stretching across the floor.

Roses aren't the only climbers, of course. Who could do without clematis to dress up a daphne in midsummer, or extend the season of a climbing rose, for that matter? There are fragrant honeysuckles and hydrangeas, polygonums and pyracanthas. Nothing better can happen to a Norway maple than to have some English ivy wander up its trunk. The list of fine climbers is a long one. With only the slightest training any of them will knit together a garden, softening the hard edges and teaching the gardener a thing or two along the way.

Every year I participate in a plant and seed exchange, which, although small and distinctly unsophisticated, is one of my favorite spring rituals. The event started up some years ago when my friend Kit, a gardener across town, arrived one day to claim some vinca I wanted to get rid of. He brought with him a box full of annual seedlings—dahlias, lobelias, some saponarias. He raises an assortment of plants each winter, and I have been the happy recipient of his excess. One year it was a clump of *Trifolium repens quadrifolia purpurascens*, which had come from a prize-winning exhibit at the Chelsea Flower Show in England. Last year he arrived with a tray full of annual forget-me-nots.

How he chooses his plants is not clear to me. Once he had nothing but blue-flowered selections. Another year he might include plants with long and complicated names that appeal to his sense of the exotic. I am glad to have them, no matter what. We follow their progress through the summer with occasional phone calls and visits. The All-America selection committee wouldn't think much of our tabulations, but we carry on as if we were engaged in science.

For my part of the exchange, I select plants that don't fit or thrive in my garden, plus those that must be divided. Aconitums have come and gone, likewise lavender, roses, azaleas, hostas, lilies, irises—you name it. One of the benefits of having a plant grow to mature size is the chance of sharing slivers of it with your friends.

There are numerous plant exchanges with goals more high-minded than the simple passing of a plant from one friend to another. The North American Rock Garden Society annually offers seeds in an undertaking that is as enormous and complicated as the plants are choice. If you become a member of the Royal Horticultural Society of England, you will receive as part of your membership privileges its list of excess seeds from the gardens at Wisley, allying yourself with gardeners around the world.

Despite their simple origins, these swaps and exchanges have kept alive important strains of plants that otherwise might become extinct. On a local level, plants such as the Gilfeather turnip might have been lost except for the trading nature of Vermont gardeners. On a national scale, the Seed-Savers Exchange in Iowa protects a vast number of plants from being lost. No matter how inconsequential the loss, gardeners can't stand the notion of another gardener losing a plant, for whatever resaon. When an Alaskan freeze moved down and crushed the Northwest a couple years ago, swapping allowed gardeners there to replenish their borders with the tender plants that are the pride of the region. Gardeners who had one or another specimen in a greenhouse or cold frame helped out those whose plants had perished. Some of the replacements came from friends in the Southeast. Little was lost altogether.

The plants that have been passed into my garden are mostly regular fare: an Alaskan fern from a friend in Oregon, potentillas and peonies from a South Carolina gardener, *Iris cristata* from a new acquaintance in Virginia. And this spring a Vermonter left me a boxwood grown to perfection in a simple but elegant pot. He has also promised me a snippet of a handsomely variegated pulmonaria. I am mulling over what to give him in return.

A plant is valuable in a garden, not simply for its flowers, its foliage, its form, its fragrance. Sometimes it is most valuable because of the people and places it represents. Any plant of the most pedestrian pedigree can fill the bill. But no garden should be without such associations.

One of the rewards of not worrying much about the lawn is that the lawn goes on with its own life, now and then providing the gardener with pleasant surprises. The lush beauty of my lawn these days is an unexpected delight. For the past five months it has been a dingy, threadbare affair, lumpy and bruised by the winter. But now it is a rich dark green from end to end, a smooth, gently undulating sward that sparkles with dew in the morning and is streaked with shadows at day's end. The public relations people from any of the grass-seed companies would applaud this lawn in spring.

It would be nice if the lawn remained a perfect green from spring to winter. I have tried on occasion to achieve such verdant perfection. I once kept a smaller lawn, one that needed only ten minutes' mowing. I turned over the tired old grass and amended the soil, then sowed the finest seed and laid down a light layer of straw. I fed and limed and watered the young turf. I even bought a manual aerator to open the pores of the soil. I would proceed around the lawn with this bright-orange, oversize fork, driving it into the ground and giving it a wiggle with every insertion. Despite these efforts, by the second year the lawn looked only slightly more refined than it had originally. So I decided my present lawn would have to survive without constant attention.

From the end of April until the end of June, and again in September and October, the lawn grows to perfection. Mowing is a nearly constant—and always pleasant—task. The grass grows thickly; it feels springy yet firm underfoot, like the finest carpet you can buy. The tire tracks of my mower run across it like ribbons, outlining the broad stripes made by the mower blade. There is a simple and satisfying rhythm to the work. The steady hum of the mower surrounds me as I dream about the prospects for the garden.

Soon, however, dandelions will dot the lawn, appearing suddenly and sending up their radiant yellow blooms. Like the crocuses that flower before them, the dandelions disappear quickly. I don't worry much about their presence. Occasionally my wife and I make an effort to dig them out, but more often we simply enjoy them. My three-year-old daughter picks them for all sorts of occasions—for her, a lawn without a small colony of dandelions loses much of its appeal.

In the heat of high summer the lawn becomes weary and reveals other aspects of its personality. As the turf becomes parched, the outline of what we imagine is the foundation of an old barn or the remains of a stone wall begins to appear, the way early versions of a painting sometimes rise up through the succeeding layers of paint. Someday I am going to dig up the area. Perhaps a course of good fieldstone lies there, covered by the thin skin of soil. Elsewhere patches of the lawn stay noticeably green. I imagine they mark spots where trees or shrubs once grew, their vacant holes now filled with rich loam.

For now, though, the lawn is full of activity. The worms are hard at work, tunneling through the soil and the birds are in concentrated pursuit of the worms. The thirsty roots of silver and Norway maples are on the move, extending into new territory in search of water. The lawn may seem a simple frame to the glory of the garden, but it has a vibrant life of its own.

The appearance of a garden emerging from the still cool soil in spring and that of a child rising out of a warm bed on most any day are not entirely dissimilar. I am reasonably acquainted with both children and gardens. No matter what the day may bring for the child—laughter, tears, victories, meltdowns—he or she awakens with a look and air of calm: fragile yet full of energy. The garden also unfurls itself gently, with a restrained vigor and a deceptive look of perfection. In the child at daybreak and the garden at ground break, the promise of perfection is soon dented by many forces, natural and otherwise. The peonies will likely have their stems broken in various places; rose canes will reach out and scratch the gardener's face; once-neat mounds of foliage will exhaust themselves in a fit of flowering and collapse in ramshackle heaps of stem and tattered flower. The day or the season is never very old before a guiding hand is needed.

In the garden, this guiding hand takes the form of supports of all shapes and sizes. I have assembled a collection of these devices over the years. I have a standard assortment of bamboo stakes, long and short, in thicknesses from that of a pencil to that of my thumb. There are a few peony hoops, or rings, as some people call them—circular metal grids mounted on four legs. Somewhere along the way, I invested heavily in linking stakes, the willowy metal rods with crooked necks that hook to one another. Each spring I also save gleanings from the pruning work on the willows, lilacs, dogwoods, and such. And obviously you cannot be without a certain number of tall and hefty rebar rods if you wish to see your heleniums and asters standing in the fall.

The important factor in this matter is not the type of supports you use, but how you handle them. Most plants require sturdier corseting than one might imagine. It does no good, however, to keep your plants upright if they look as though they're doing it against their will. A tall, well-fed helenium in full flower wants almost a truss of girders; penstemons want only the touch of a pea vine to survive until fall. In short, it takes the cool head of an engineer and a magician's sleight of hand to stake plants so that they can weather a July torrent in full bloom, all the while holding a pose that is natural, even advantageous.

There is more engineer than artist in my blood, and my staking jobs often look more like scaffolding for a building than support for a plant. I start with the peonies, which demand a strong hand because of their thin ankles. ('Festiva Maxima' is the most challenging; it gets a ring of bamboo and an interior cat's cradle of jute.) Then I move to the geraniums and nepetas, which need only light bolstering. The large filipendula always needs a sturdy stake or two; and some of the campanulas and platycodons like a bit of railing to sprawl on if there isn't a more upright plant nearby. I continue throughout the summer, staking certain plants as their flower stalks shoot up, adding height to some stakes, clipping back others. Late in the season I tether *Miscanthus sinensis* 'Zebrinus' so that it will stand through autumn and on into winter. Keeping a child upright through the trials of a single day is not so simple a task, of course. But in either case if the job is well done—with respect for the character of plant or person—the results will be rewarding, if not always what you expected at the start.

Looking directly away from our kitchen door, you see the vegetable garden. Like any vegetable garden, ours has a look of the familiar and the common. There are orderly rows of recognizable leaf shapes and colors: the broad sprawling ones of squash, the heart-shaped simplicity of beans, the soft filigree of carrots, and the hollow reeds of young onions. At this point in the season, largely free of weeds and still full of promise, it is a scene brimming with the life force.

For five months of the year, however, it is not much to look at. From late fall to early spring it is a lumpy stubble-strewn expanse, the unshaven cheek of a disheveled season. To spruce up the place a bit, in summer as well as winter, we have been gradually adding bits of ornament to it. First I surrounded it with a yew hedge, or more precisely, with a picket of scrawny young plants that will, someday, having gorged on compost and 5-10-5, fill out into a low dense hedge, marking the garden's outline in the winter and keeping it safe from soccer balls and free-ranging toddlers the rest of the year. Dissecting the ground into various beds are paths lined with old tiles unearthed from the garage. Stones that we turn up through the year are set into the spaces between the tiles. The combination of stones and tiles makes a pleasant mosaic and keeps us from having to haul the rocks to some other more distinct spot.

During the summer a standard bay tree stands at the center of the garden, surrounded by pots of annuals. Some of the raised beds contain flowers for cutting. As in many other vegetable gardens, this plot also has some of the best soil on the property, receives the most consistent sunlight, and is the hands-down favorite part of the garden for our two children. They enjoy cutting flowers from the borders but would prefer to settle down and eat a whole row of young carrots fresh from the ground.

As a means of supplying our family with green goods through the summer, the vegetable garden is a miserable failure. The problem is not its size—twenty feet long by fifteen feet wide—but the erratic and impractical style of the owners and operators. We plant not according to government guidelines for a healthy, well-balanced diet or to assure ourselves a stocked larder in January (though there are always plenty of potatoes). Our tactics are guided by our stomachs, the siren songs of catalog writers, a desire to succeed, and an interest in having our children join in the process. Like the tactics that brought low the economy of the former Soviet Union (and may yet topple this household), our garden follows grand schemes (mesclun as the cure for all ills) and pet passions ("I like 'Sweet 100' tomatoes, and I see nothing wrong with having six plants for a family of four"). There is little room left for logic.

The addition of ornament, however, and a bit of hedging surely introduce an appearance of order to this garden. Some days I am even tempted to refer to it as a kitchen garden, that refined cousin of the simple vegetable garden. Still, there is no denying the essential nature of vegetable gardens—a tendency toward self-indulgence, disorder, revolution. Come July, I imagine there will be tomatoes spilling over the top of the hedge, and the walks will be lost beneath a tide of squash, bush beans, and other plants that are indispensable to the sensible and satisfactory operation of a vegetable garden.

Over time most gardeners accumulate a sizable assortment of clay pots, although the forces of acquisition are offset by the forces of clumsiness (dropping pots on the brick walk), foolishness (leaving them out after the arrival of hard frosts), and simple old age, so the number never increases as quickly as you might expect. My own collection runs the gamut from a dozen or so two-inch pots to a few two-foot containers, with a large number of pots in differing sizes and varying degrees of ornamentation in between. How I've come to have so many tiny pots is a mystery. I rarely use them; but there is a look of solid utility about them, and I never pass the neat little stacks without a slight sense of well-being, the way a cook might feel about a shelf lined with jars of preserves.

The development in the middle of the nineteenth century of machines to mass-produce pots all but eliminated the many potteries that made them by hand. These days, however, the world is rich in good handmade pots. In the last decade a number of potters here and abroad have begun to produce classic designs by traditional methods. Now you can buy a Long Tom or a wickerweave design or a basic pot with a simple rolled rim. There are brightly colored pots for sunny and Mediterranean climates, and vast tubs for folks with large plants or dreams of Versailles. You also can find the traditional ringed terra-rossa pots from Italy, with their slightly irregular but sturdy good looks and a pale coloring that seems ageless and looks at home anywhere.

Almost anything will grow in a pot, and in many cases plants will flourish in the coddled climate, watered and fed to their hearts' content. The process of matching pot to plant or vice versa is not a small or slight matter. There is an individuality to each pot that calls for a certain plant. Unlike the planting of something in a border, where the job is a mechanical one of preparing the soil and getting the plant in at the right depth, the planting of something in a pot is more like arranging a marriage.

There are no guarantees, however, that you will avoid disaster. The troubles are not always the ones familiar to gardeners, but they are no less numerous. Setting aside drought or malnourishment—which are Acts of the Gardener, not Acts of God—you have to worry about unexpected winds that arrive from an unusual direction with great force to topple standards and top-heavy plants. More predictable but no less terrifying is the daily arrival of the newspaper, flung from the open window of a moving van. Last summer errant dailies upended a pot of hosta and snapped off two stands of lilies just approaching perfection on our porch. Visiting dogs knock over containers in the excitement of greetings, though not so often as visiting and resident children, all of whom move through the world without ever looking where they are going.

No matter how lucky you are at keeping your pots whole and healthy, you can never have enough, for there are always more plants to grow, plants that for one reason or another call for a clay pot. A pot made by hand and mottled and colored with the signs of age, however, is handsome in its own right. Good pots add an element of earthy architecture to porches and terraces, and their reappearance each spring gives a sense of continuity to the changing years.

In order to examine something like a crocus or a species tulip, my two-year-old daughter likes to lie flat out on her stomach. When the first clump of crocuses began to bloom in one corner of the lawn last month, I called her over for a look. She came over, stood for a moment, then dropped all the way to the ground, where I joined her. This is a good vantage point for viewing such plants, and since it was sunny and warm but with a slight breeze in the air, lying on the ground was certainly the best place to be in the garden. On hands and knees we circled the small cluster of crocuses, a standard yellow-flowered form, and then rested. At a time of year when there is so much to do, when the strongest urge is to race around, it was pleasant to indulge in such slow study.

There is nothing new in this approach to looking at a plant; at one time or another many people spend time with their noses at soil level in order to consider the subtle charms of some specimen. The encyclopedic Thomas H. Everett thought nothing of crawling around on the ground to get a good look at a plant; this method must account, in part, for his great understanding of plants. English gardener and writer Christopher Lloyd likes to take a blanket out into a corner of his garden to write and relax.

Every garden should include in its design some places that invite lounging. Gardens are nothing if they are not relaxing. Ideally, I suppose, such a spot should offer a fresh view of some aspect of the place. In my last garden one of my favorite stopping spots was under the low-hanging branches of a cluster of hemlocks, which sat on a bit of ground slightly elevated above the rest of the garden. Tucked under the hemlocks' branches were a minute terrace of fieldstone and a simple bench. Seen from the garden, the bench appeared too much in the open, too exposed. But when you sat on it, back under the shadows of the hemlocks, a sense of shelter prevailed. At the end of the day I liked to relax there, savoring the long shadows. I particularly liked to sit there during a summer rain; the branches kept me dry and hung even lower, shrouding my view and changing my perspective of the garden.

In my present garden there are a number of good stopping spots. In one area a shrub border juts out into the lawn, hiding in its lee a small green eddy with a bench. Across the lawn in another corner, the bottommost branch of a ginkgo calls for a swing of some sort. There is talk of enclosing the vegetable garden with a stone wall. Built solidly and to the right height, a stone wall begs passersby to sit. Actually you don't so much sit on a stone wall as pause or give your feet a rest.

For an extended break, the lawn is still the best option. In my case, the ground drops away from the house for a couple feet before leveling out. This slight banking makes a perfect place to lounge. When I'm exhausted and unable to move or just befuddled and unable to figure out where to place some plant, I like to stretch out against this grassy incline and consider my options.

JUNE

A NURSERYMAN IS AN ACROBAT OF UNCOMMON ABILITIES, and the feats he performs makes the efforts of a conventional circus performer look like a Sunday drive in the country. Barnum and Bailey's acrobats practice a few set routines day after day. The nurseryman enjoys none of this security. The plants and products that make up his act vary with the seasons. He has a full-time job just keeping up with the changes—deciding which new items deserve a chance in his store, which do not. He must constantly be testing "new" plants to find out if they are new, if the "delicate red" of an introduction is red or actually a muddy orange.

When he is not dealing with these matters, the nurseryman is dealing with the customers, who demand of him a different though not unrelated set of skills—those of the fortune-teller. From the most meager evidence he divines answers to every sort of gardening question. Looking at a brown and withered leaf, he identifies the plant it came from and the malady it suffers; reading a plan hastily sketched on a breakfast napkin, he produces a planting scheme for a site unseen. He can translate the word "whatchamacallit" (as well as many others like it) and point a customer to the proper tool and away from certain trouble.

What really sets the nurseryman apart from these other performers, I think, is not so much his skill as his partner. He works with as willful and capricious a character as you can find—the weather. Going into business with the heavens requires a leap of faith as bold and difficult as any. To say the least, he cannot always anticipate his partner's next move. If the nurseryman plans a festive June weekend, say, to herald the arrival of summer and the gardening season, he stands an excellent chance of getting rain (or worse), while summer sits in a bus station somewhere, reading the sports page. If the next year the nurseryman moves his opening forward to a weekend when the weather is sure to be well-behaved, then he can almost certainly count on a once-in-a-decade freak hailstorm come Saturday morning.

To be fair, the nurseryman owes much of his good fortune to the weather, for there is nothing like a sunny, warm Saturday morning to bring out the gardener in everybody. As anyone who has sat housebound through a long winter knows, a visit to a garden center is a special event; the excitement one feels is not unlike the thrill of a visit to the circus. The smell of peat moss and fir bark fills the air. There are more plants than one can remember ever seeing (and always more squash plants and crimson rhododendrons than necessary). People mill about, many of them struggling under piles of seedlings and supplies, most of which they never intended to buy when they left the house.

And if you're hunting for the owner, take a look over behind the sales counter. He's the fellow making change for a twenty with one hand, giving a quick lesson in pruning with the other hand, and nodding someone else in the direction of the lawn supplies. It's a performance that by itself makes the trip worthwhile.

It is a long-standing point of honor among gardeners never to step outside without a pocketknife, no matter what the occasion or the destination. The pocketknife certainly deserves this reputation, for a single blade can manage miracles in the hands of a skillful operator. All the same, many gardens might be better off if their owners devoted as much time and effort to a garden journal, an equally simple and versatile tool.

In the strict sense of the term, a garden journal is a personal account of any and all proceedings that take place in a garden through the years. The particular purpose of these notebooks is as varied as the gardeners themselves. A journal may serve as a record book, a photo album, an order form immune from the pinch of a checkbook, a bulletin board for posting reminders.

Here a gardener can assemble the lily garden of a lifetime, pray to the heavens for better—or at least different—weather, sketch plans, curse cats. Taken together, these entries chronicle the slow and meandering evolution of a garden.

My own journal has taken different shapes over the years. For a time, I logged notes on loose sheets of plain white paper, which I then gathered together with order forms, used seed packets, plant labels, photographs, and muddied pieces of graph paper bearing the smudged remains of past garden plans, and chucked everything into a manila folder. The pleasant result of this haphazard method was that while rummaging through past bank statements I would come across small pieces of paper reminding me to order a certain astilbe or detailing a forgotten account of one afternoon's work: "April 16 (Patriot's Day): Turned six and a half bales of peat into the lower garden, hoping to improve its health, and then drank beer in hopes of upgrading mine."

I abandoned this free-form approach not long ago and purchased a rather grand volume, bound in leather and guaranteed to fulfill my every need for the next five years. This diary (as its publisher calls it) looked entirely unsuited to gardens or gardeners, but a month or two after it arrived I pulled it out in desperation. We have performed our respective duties, I writing, it receiving, for some time now, and I am getting accustomed to this newcomer, though I can't say we're a perfect pair. All the days are allotted the same amount of space, Monday through Sunday, week in and week out, an arrangement that doesn't match my habits at all. There are months when if I write anything it's a bitter complaint about the weather; and there are other seasons when every day demands a couple of pages, to say nothing of the space I need for pasting in photographs. The publisher views each day with equal affection, yet I have never met two days I felt the same way about. Furthermore, there is no way this crisply bound volume can accommodate the accumulated paper I need to keep nearby. A garden journal must serve as a time capsule for a special breed of pack rat.

All the same, it offers plenty of that essential ingredient, paper. Like a good garden knife, a gardener's journal depends on its owner for its virtuosity, the quality of its product. Without that it amounts to nothing more than a blank pile of stationery.

One of the most remarkable sights at the Chelsea Flower Show in London occurs on the afternoon of the final day. At 5:00 P.M. the exhibitors are allowed to sell all the plants in their displays. Everything goes on the block and must be carted away by the closing bell at 5:30, some of it with the help of a friend or perhaps a child's toy wagon. Most buyers, lacking mechanical advantage but fortified by the excitement of their acquisitions, simply carry them like bags of groceries, peering through the foliage to find their way. The result of all this commotion is a parade of people smothered beneath splendid specimen plants—full-blooming hydrangeas, glorious spikes of delphiniums, billowing chamaecyparis. To many onlookers it is a queer and unlikely sight, but in truth it's only slightly strange; gardeners have enjoyed this restless state for a long time. They are forever moving something from here to there and, generally, back again.

Although we ran out of space for new plants some time ago, you couldn't have guessed it by watching the activity in our yard this spring. Plants were shifted from this garden to that one and replaced by others. Some moved just a foot or so. The winter's dead were buried and replaced. A large lilac took the place of a small mountain laurel that blistered and perished during a cold snap in February. In all these changes we had the aid of a new wheelbarrow, a handsome and sturdy machine that came to us as a gift. The side panels are removable and its wooden wheel is wrapped with a steel band, which quickly took on a pleasant rusty patina. Rolling along our walk it clatters like an old hay wagon. I never imagined the need for such a tool in a small yard, but after a few months I am assured that a wheelbarrow can perform plenty of work in a postage-stamp place like ours.

Like most simple tools, the wheelbarrow has changed little over the centuries. Some lacked sides or had particularly long handles (to allow the operator to transport water without tilting the container too much), while others were constructed of cast iron or with three wheels. That master gardener Thomas Jefferson experimented with the efficiency of different designs. Basically, though, the wheelbarrow has remained a first cousin not far removed from the earliest "wilbarewe," which was mentioned sometime around 1340.

The arrival of our wheelbarrow had much the same effect that a new car has on a teenager. Suddenly we discovered a long list of tasks that required a wheelbarrow, most of them chores we had been quietly avoiding. The bricks we had saved for edging a bed of iris were trundled out and put in place. I finally removed a moldering mass of wood chips from the driveway and spread them out among the shrubs, where they belonged. With one side panel taken off, the wheelbarrow became an excellent mobile platform for potting up the annuals that we put around our front door and terrace. I know that I might also fill it with potted plants and park it in the yard as a piece of ornament; but I can't see letting such a useful tool stand idle while there is so much work going on.

Most people don't choose to have shade in their gardens, they just end up with it. Either they inherit a garden hidden beneath tall trees or their property is shaded by a neighboring house. Our shade is mostly the work of some pin oaks and maples that cluster at the southwestern corner of our yard. They are the legacy of someone I never knew. The trees stand forty feet tall, maybe more. Their branches merge into one another, creating an arboreal highway for a community of squirrels and casting long, luxurious shadows across the lawn and gardens.

There are all sorts and degrees of shade. There is morning shade, which isn't great, and there is afternoon shade, which can be. Stygian gloom is no good for growing things, nor is dank shade, which rots plants (and probably gardeners, too). Gardeners refer to half shade and full shade, to high shade and filtered sunlight. If you want to grow vegetables, you want no shade, but otherwise you might like a full dose of morning sun followed by dappled afternoon shade, the kind cast by a honey locust. The subtleties go on endlessly, and any gardener who deals in the subject will offer a different definition—and different solutions—for any kind of shade.

Some gardeners will tell you that shade is a blessing, to be desired. However, most are apt to disagree, even if they don't care about growing corn. At the end of our first summer in the shade I began to mumble about cutting down a tree. My wife quickly and quite rightly convinced me that I was foolish to make such threats. These trees give our flat piece of land a sense of height as well as a look of maturity that is otherwise impossible to have in a young garden. They nicely hide the neighbors' house through the summer. At night the broad canopies rustle in the wind, and in fall they carpet the ground in shades of red, orange, gold, and yellow, making up for some of the color they have stolen during the summer months.

We did have a tree specialist open up the crowns of the trees, but that hasn't changed the essential character of the place. There is ample shade. In the corner where the trees are grouped, little light gets through once the leaves are out. Farther out in the yard sunlight filters down in agreeable quantities. Patches of sun appear here and there, bathing a bit of the lawn or some plants for a brief spell and then disappearing. It's not enough for a tan, barely enough for a lawn. All the same, there is no end of plants that thrive on this meager offering. I have a growing fondness for ferns, with their graceful shapes and varied rich greens. Likewise bergenias, whose large glossy leaves gleam in the half-light as do the yellow-leaved and variegated plants such as hostas and Solomon's seal. The nodding white flowers of Japanese anemones stand out in the shadows of late summer.

A garden in shade is a different kind of garden from one soaked in sun. There's little that's grand and much that's fleeting. You won't find the brilliant colors of a rose bed, but you will find rich, dark shadows and a sense of coolness and calm. You won't often hear a visitor gasp in awe; you may hear a contented murmur. And you may find the gardener just standing there, admiring a lone shaft of sunlight come to rest on the lawn.

Sometime this month we will get a good drenching rainstorm that will topple one or two of our few lupine blooms and remind me that I never finished staking, tying, and otherwise supporting various plants in the garden. You can't blame the plants for needing this attention; it's not in their nature to stand at attention for four or five months, especially with the enormous flowers some of them must carry. And it's not a demanding task if you get to it early enough; the plants, as usual, will let you know what they need.

You can choose your own tools. Many gardeners use nothing but small twigs and branches, selecting the particular piece of brush according to the need—assorted twigs, say, for a sprawly geranium, or a bigger and stouter branch for a delphinium or thalictrum. If you set out your brush early on, the leaves of the plants will gradually envelop the supports, cloaking them in return for their assistance. In some gardens in early spring, where the gardeners are on top of their jobs (and not waiting for the lupine to crash before they go to work), you will find the beds dotted with these small thickets. It's a nice way to see the garden before everything fills in, and the sense of security is reassuring.

This method appeals to me in principle, and I have admired it in many gardens. In my own garden I've never used it much or with much success. I constructed a nice rigging for some aconitum once. They rose up through the brush according to plan and kept on growing, way above the tallest of my branches. Then they grew spindly and flopped over. I decided the problem was the soil—not the supports—and moved the plants.

Despite that discouraging attempt I still use the modest amount of brush we generate. But it's not enough or of the right sort for the jobs that need attention. So I keep a quiver of bamboo stakes plus some green metal wands. And plenty of twine, for playing cat's cradle throughout the garden: supporting the billowy blooms of a peony, persuading a climbing rose cane in one direction along a fence, keeping the arching branches of spireas from bowing too low and smothering a bed of Japanese irises.

The best solution is to use sturdy plants that withstand the weather and the weight of their own flowers without an elaborate superstructure. The list is long but not consistent from garden to garden. What stands tall in one spot is spineless in another. In that case you can always hope that it will be bolstered up by stronger neighbors. A once-straggling *Geranium endressii* now makes a fine mound hemmed in by stands of hostas and daylilies. A clump of lythrum does most of the work of supporting some tall lilies—and makes a fine arrangement in the process.

I don't worry about all the lilies in our garden. I once planted a couple dozen of them in a shady area with the thought they would naturalize among the other plants, providing bright splashes of color against hollies and rhododendrons. Unfortunately, the overarching trees offered more shade than I admitted, and the lilies leaned precariously toward the light. For a summer or two I tethered them to stakes. But every bit of growth above a tie was bent and tortured looking. In the end I stopped staking and now let them bend almost to the ground. I prefer the way they hover there. Their gold, yellow, and red flowers sparkle against the cover of English ivy. It's not a traditional stand of lilies, but the plants are happier (or so they seem), and it leaves me free to attend to the poor lupines.

Despite three school years spent mired in Latin textbooks and another two sorting out French, I still stumble over a good many plant names. Certain of the finest old roses, for instance, bear names that confound me. I doubt that I will ever grow them, as it's difficult to get along with plants whose names you can't pronounce. I can manage such roses as 'Roseraie de l'Hay' and 'Madame Grégoire Staechelin'. I'll shy away from 'Duchesse d'Angouleme', 'Zigeunerknabe', and 'Duc de Guiche'. They may smell exquisite, but keeping their names straight would wear me out.

In truth, the size and aspect of our garden won't allow these glorious roses; we limit ourselves to a collection of easily named climbers, some English roses, a couple rugosas, and a sturdy 'Betty Prior'. Our expanding collection of clematises, however, could soon exceed my linguistic skills. I was reminded of this the other night while reading Christopher Lloyd's reissued classic, *Clematis*. In his pronunciation guide, Lloyd tells of an overheard conversation in which one person mentioned *Clematis* 'Etoile Violette', " . . . whereupon the other person looked puzzled and asked what had a clematis to do with property leases? Was the name a joke? Following a lengthy conversation at cross-purposes (in a noisy public bar) the matter was resolved. The listener had been convinced the plant was called 'A Twelve Year Let'."

Lloyd straightens out much clematis terminology in no uncertain terms, including how to handle the generic name itself ("unequivocably CLEM-atis, with a short *e* and the accent on the first syllable") and the impenetrable 'Cholmondeley' ("pronounced Chumley"). But many pronunciation pitfalls lie before and after clematis in even a limited alphabet of plants. Take the bergenia, a bold, easygoing plant, and easily pronounced, you might think. I had always said burr-JEEN-ee-a with confidence. But I recently discovered I had had it wrong all along. Burr-GEEN-ee-a appears to be more correct. This causes me to pause now whenever I mention the plant, but I am a happy to be getting the name right (if indeed I am).

Should you worry about any of this? Not terribly, unless you run with a crowd that insists on perfect pronunciation (and in that case you might consider taking up with a new group of friends). Yet there is a need for getting at least the fundamentals right. Daunting as they may seem, the Latin terms are actually a useful shorthand, allowing gardeners of any language to know that they are talking about the same plant.

If you insist on knowing the full and correct names of every plant in your garden and you have a memory like mine, you will need labels. Originally I stuck in labels all over the place. But the frost and the squirrels upended many of them, and the garden took on the look of a rundown cemetery. As I am growing plants, not labels, I decided to note the plants and their positions in my garden diary and throw out the labels. I think the place looks better for the change, though I may not remember the exact name of a cultivar, much less whether it needs an umlaut or an *accent aigue*. I may only be able to tell offhand that the shrub by the front of the garden is a cotoneaster. That's co-TONE-ee-aster, not COTTON-easter.

Deciding where a plant should go is a complicated and trying business. A gardener can spend an entire day trying to get one plant in the ground, wandering around aimlessly, digging and refilling a number of holes. Like a dog that circles and circles to locate *the* spot to rest, my garden design is one part work and two parts walking around. I start and finish the day with a slow tour of the garden, interrupted by constant stops to imagine the placement of this or that. In the horticultural equivalent of tai chi, I draw each plant in the air.

Almost two hundred plants arrived on our doorstep this spring—annuals, perennials, shrubs, and trees. Because of the large number of plants and the small amount of time (roughly from 6 P.M. Friday to 7 P.M. Sunday, with time out for meals, child care, and assorted errands), I spent many hours considering their proper placement. But by the end of the first day, my plans lay in tatters. One small change of mind would set off a chain reaction of adjustments. The decision to put the *Astrantia major* to the right, not the left, of a certain peony, for example, meant that, two hundred feet away, a rose was suddenly homeless.

One must keep in mind at all times that the scruffy twig in one's hand will grow to be something much bigger and may even become a menace. This point is easily and conveniently forgotten. There may appear to be plenty of room in one spot for an additional plant, but most likely there isn't. I thought, for instance, that a gaping hole between a pair of junipers would be perfect for a variegated dogwood and concocted various reasons for the perfection of this arrangement. But, no, the dogwood will spread to five feet in a flash, the junipers will fill out, and the viburnum off in the distance will eventually expand into the opening I so badly wanted to fill.

Surprises below ground also thwarted my plans. One long stretch of open ground hid the substantial stumps of what must have been a dense grove of maples and oaks. Seen through the windows in winter, the area appeared clear and ready for planting. However, I soon found that any open space contained some remnant of these trees. No spot could be considered until the soil had been poked and prodded with a garden fork. If you want to know the reason for the random arrangement of chamaecyparis in the far corner of the garden, it has to do with an unseen stump nearly three feet in diameter. If the conifers look good against the roses, that's largely by chance.

Despite such obstacles, most of my deliberations involve the personal choices of what looks best where. A plant can move around quite a bit before settling. One itinerant plant that shifted around this spring was a *Miscanthus sinensis* 'Zebrinus'. It started at the entrance to the garden next to a purple-leaved smokebush. But I decided the grass, which has a floppy habit, wanted a less-conspicuous site. So I moved it next to a 'Shasta' viburnum to contrast with that plant's horizontal branching habit. But on the other side of the grass was a broom, which was also feathery and had a similar habit. I therefore moved the grass next to a clump of clethra backed by some dark-green conifers and not far from that smokebush. I moved the smokebush too, on second thought.

Summer colds make no sense. They are a contradiction in terms and contrary to all warm-blooded logic. Colds come from going around in winter without mittens or a hat; they have no place in summer. To a gardener, a cold in summer is a particularly cruel trick, for that is the time the garden unfurls new fragrances almost by the hour.

Many people mark the arrival of summer with the perfumed blossoms of the roses. Now, some gardeners will tell you the rose has lost its fragrance. That is true in the case of certain modern roses, but others, such as 'Mister Lincoln', will impress even a congested critic. The English roses developed by David Austin offer a range of perfumes. I grow five, and they are all strongly scented. Gardeners are also rediscovering the old roses and their antique elegance and distinctive perfumes. Many flower but once each summer, yet in their time they lace the air with hints of apple, myrrh, orange, spice, and lemon. A garden should not be without a rugosa rose or two, either. Many flower more than once, and all that I know are richly scented.

The season for fragrance in the garden starts well before the roses, of course, and stretches long after them. It begins in my garden with the witch hazels and moves on to *Viburnum ×bodnantense* 'Dawn' and *Daphne mezereum* 'Alba', by which time the bulbs are blooming. My favorite spring bulb this year was a narcissus, a commoner named 'Trevithian' whose yellow flowers carried a noticeable lemony scent. It overlapped with *Viburnum carlesii*, whose great white flower heads emit a fog of fragrance that moves around one end of the garden, so that you encounter it at different places, depending on which way the wind is blowing. This early, cool part of spring is especially nice because scents linger through the day. In midsummer the sun burns away most fragrance by late morning, leaving only a slight reminder at day's end.

One of my favorite scents in the early-summer garden belongs to the boxwood. Many people cannot stomach the smell, but I have always relished the sharp rich odor, which suggests to me the formality, maturity, and luxuriance of gardens in Europe, California, and the South. As a plant boxwood is unremarkable, but as a stimulus of the imagination it is provocative.

The perfume of lilac inspires recollections for anyone who has lived in New England for any length of time. My wife and I inherited a dozen lilacs with our garden, and their scent is one we now almost take for granted, like the salt breeze at the seashore. But the smell of lilac is like spring—fresh, sweet, and delicate. Each year I am delighted by the rich-purple blooms sagging off the branches, and I regret that they last such a short time.

By the time the lilacs go by, however, our garden is filled with other smells. If I brush a stand of *Geranium macrorrhizum*, my hand takes on the flavor of a pungent citrus. The tiny leaves of a gold-edged thyme want ruffling too, as do those of a nearby *Calamintha nepeta*. This plant smells of spearmint, and its leaves remain redolent through the winter, much like lavender, whose tattered gray leaves give up faded reminders of high summer even in the depths of February.

Even the smallest piece of ground offers innumerable prospects for growing plants, and the longer one lives on a property, the more these hiding places reveal themselves. A nongardener might look at a site and see room for a swatch of lawn, perhaps a flower bed of some sort, and some foundation plantings. The gardener, on the other hand, can hardly take a step or turn his or her head without spotting some space into which a plant could be stuck or some vertical surface on which something could clamber. In our garden, the prospects seem to be increasing rather than decreasing, and I am starting to worry that we will never catch up with the essential planting duties that present themselves.

Among the areas needing attention is a two-hundred-foot length of wooden fence backing a mixed border. The weathered wood of the fence is nice enough unadorned, but it would look much better covered with roses, ivies, clematis, and maybe a *Schizophragma hydrangeoides*. Two ivies are already in place, and this spring I have also planted an *Ampelopsis brevipedunculata* 'Elegans', a 'New Dawn' rose, and a climbing hydrangea, which will have the run of a twenty-foot stretch.

Across the lawn from this fence is the garage, whose gray stucco walls also call out for plants. The plan is to espalier a fruit tree on the south side. But what of the other three blank sides? Their surfaces would nicely complement most any plant. Elsewhere in the garden there are other fences, a couple of sturdy hedges, and various trees—all of them candidates for a drapery of some sort. This is to say nothing of the house, bare except for a lone wisteria trained to one flank.

At the ground level, too, there are countless nooks and crannies waiting to be filled. The aging lilacs ought to have something shading their roots. Early-blooming shrubs like spireas, mountain laurels, andromedas, and rhododendrons offer the perfect cover for foliage plants such as epimediums or wild ginger to keep them company through the summer.

The most neglected areas around here are the foundation plantings. Along the north side of the house sits a collection of evergreens, mostly conifers, which are too big for the space they occupy. Many of them must come out if the few gems are to survive. Besides, the house is slowly growing mossy in their shade. Their removal will provide a great opportunity to add new plants. But which ones and in what arrangement? I decided early in the year to defer this decision until the confusion of spring had passed and I could ponder things in the slower days of summer.

Meanwhile there are seeds that need sowing in the vegetable garden and annuals to pop into spots where spring bulbs have finished their performance. There is one small bed that is going to be planted with either lavender or dianthus, and I need to decide which one. Furthermore, the layout of this garden calls for a boxwood hedge to divide the front and back portions. When the boxwood goes in, it would probably be the sensible time to plant a crab apple in the empty nook by the back steps. If we had any more land than our present postage stamp, I imagine we would have to hire a gardener to keep up with the planting.

JULY

FOR MIDSUMMER FIREWORKS AND CELEBRATION, A GAR-
dener can do little better than the flowers and foliage of annuals. Annuals bring a festive spontaneity to the garden, adding
unrestrained good cheer and unflagging vitality to match the
heat and light of the season. The grand, unfurled leaves of cannas, with their bright, bawdy flowers fluttering above, or the
delicate, satiny shades of Iceland poppies are a boon to any garden, for all can use a shot of color and gaiety to carry them
through the heat of summer. And annuals can add an exotic
lushness—almost a look of the tropics—that is as invigorating
as a stand of pink flamingos.

In colder climates, the traditional definition of an annual is
expanding beyond the tried-and-true offerings to include any-

thing that can be cajoled or tricked into making a quick display. In this pursuit gardeners are being aided and abetted by the nursery folks who are offering up an ever-expanding list of tender plants from New Zealand, Australia, South Africa, and parts of South America. A great many tender plants that can't stand a northern winter (who can blame them?) now can be bought through the mail; having spent their infancy in a warmer climate, they arrive ready to revel in the summer heat. Gardeners these days think nothing of growing a range of plants from the Southern Hemisphere, the pink-and-salmon-flowered diascias, for instance, or the colorful sword-leafed phormiums. *Melianthus major*, a striking shrub from South Africa with blue-green, elegantly toothed leaves, also is finding its way into summer borders. The bold looks and flamboyant colors of these plants enliven gardens in the same way that the summer outfits of vacationers lend a cheering note to even the most northern outpost.

Nevertheless, the more commonly known and sometimes scorned annuals still add to this summer celebration. The disdain for them is undeserved, because all—from the bright, shaggy blossoms of the amaranth known as love-lies-bleeding and the colorful rays of cosmos, which bob above the crowd as though standing on stilts, to the marigolds, impatiens, salvias, and lobelias scrambling around at their feet—lift the spirits of the garden and of the gardener.

The annuals of old are also returning to gardens, looking exotic and slightly foreign even though they are simply emerging from a regrettable exile. Globe amaranth and sunflowers are two of my favorite old-timers; another is the gangly *Nicotiana sylvestris*, a striking plant of great character that bears as little resemblance to its modern kin as Uncle Sam does to Rush Limbaugh.

Any of these plants can find a place in today's borders. They are invaluable for filling gaps. Indeed, they make a virtue of gaps, and leave the gardener feeling clever rather than ashamed about those bare patches that invariably appear in spring. Many annuals and tender perennials will happily overwinter in a pot and then be sunk in the ground or stood in a place of prominence for the summer. Wherever they appear, they spark the summer garden, lending a familiar feeling of good cheer and trumpeting the return of sunny days when the cicadas sing and bright colors are the order of the day. They allow a gardener and a garden to escape the gravitational pull of their climate, at least for a few short months.

The watering can remains largely anonymous in the annals of garden technology, though so far no one has found a good reason to change its appearance except for some tinkering with colors and the addition of plastic models. As a tool ideally suited to its task, the watering can endures with good reason. It has bulk enough to transport water for a number of plants yet when loaded is not so light that one is apt to dispense the water carelessly. Attach a rosette to its neck and you can minister to the most delicate seedlings. Set aside the rosette and you can quickly attend to the needs of a row of young shrubs.

Once you master the heft of a can it is possible to deliver a fine yet steady stream into the tightest clearing. And when you finish the work you might easily put a watering can out front on display, for it makes an elegant ornament. At Hidcote Manor in England, two stout, well-tarnished watering cans stand as sentinels at one entrance to the red border, looking like old pensioners retired after many years of honorable service, yet still ready to return to duty should the need arise.

The subject of water is much on everyone's mind at this time of year. Farmers thumb through *The Old Farmer's Almanac* and scan the sky for friendly clouds. Children dream of chasing through the arching spray of lawn sprinklers, and gardeners rise early to haul hoses and tote water here and there about the yard. It makes little difference whether the season began in downpour or drought. July summons weather that is as dry as it is hot, turning a gardener's attention from pruning and such tasks to taking the temperature of his plants, for they are a temperamental bunch and will fall into a swoon if not treated with care.

No matter how many plants you have, watering takes time. It's a job for the end of the day—either one—when you can spare a few minutes to give your plants the long drink they prefer and look them over for signs of ill health. It's a simple treatment, and I realize it's possible to handle the job by computer; but I know I'd end up pacing around the garden making sure all was well, so I stick to the watering can and occasional wrestling matches with the hose.

My daughter discovered the first tomato of the year. She is six and has those youthful eyes that can spot a glimmer of red at fifty paces. The date was the second of July, and the tomato was 'Gardener's Delight', an early cherry variety. The arrival of the first fresh tomato is a cause for celebration, just as the first snowfall of winter and the bold unfurling of the first crocus flowers in spring. By the time we pluck that first tomato we will have already harvested any number of other vegetables. But a ripe tomato, well, that marks the season of high summer.

Except for a small, excited procession across the lawn and into the kitchen, we hold no ceremonies to commemorate the event. We hold no annual dance and crown no Tomato Queen. But the season would not be complete without a harvest of tomatoes. (We could, on the other hand, probably survive a year without squash.) We gauge the progress—and the success—of the summer by the tomatoes: the young strapping plants, their lanky branches dotted with yellow stars of flowers like some summer version of a Christmas tree; the branches thick with green fruits, which, we know, will shortly bow the plants and later spill them onto the ground. When the tomatoes reach their peak they color the north end of the vegetable garden a rich, rusty red.

The four plants standing squarely in one corner of the vegetable garden are an essential, though small, part of its design. Two sides of the garden are edged in a low hedge of yew. Along another side is a pergola being covered by grapes. The fourth side backs against the garage, where a pear tree is slowly being trained up the wall. Paths of rough fieldstone cut the modest plot into beds for various vegetables and herbs. In the center is an open circle that holds a different accent each year. One year we stood a standard bay tree in the space. This summer we planted a tepee of beans, providing not only a bit of visual punctuation but also a hiding place for our children.

The notion of putting together a vegetable garden that is as aesthetically pleasing as it is productive is a subject of increasing interest among gardeners. It is not a new idea, however, but rather a return to an old practice. The kitchen garden was a sophisticated art form in the Victorian era, a time when high standards and low wages combined to produce large gardens laid out with simple geometry, planted with a great variety of edible and ornamental plants and maintained with an elegant utility. Whether it was handsome brick walkways or sweet peas grown on tall tripods, art showed up everywhere in the kitchen garden.

Along with an appreciation of the layout of the kitchen garden has come a greater interest in vegetables with character— those varieties from around this country and abroad that offer distinctive flavor or looks or both. There are lettuces and greens in almost endless variety of colors and tastes. Scarlet runner beans clamber up poles; the bright colors of plants such as chards and chili peppers sparkle beside bold clumps of artichoke and rhubarb, leeks and kale. Richly colored and strikingly shaped potatoes, radishes, and turnips make digging in the ground a treasure hunt. And always there are tomatoes, from the mammoth beefsteaks to the elegant plums and the rubylike cherries. We could not do without a complement of tomatoes. They are not the most handsome part of our kitchen garden (though a tripod of sturdy plain bamboo stakes, lashed together with twine, lends a look of order), but the act of eating a tomato at the garden's edge, the fruit warm with sunshine and splattering your face with its juices, is the perfect taste for a summer day.

A new garden in midsummer produces weeds and surprises in about equal numbers. Actually, this is true only if the gardener took the time to make a plan and then had the sense to follow it. Otherwise, the surprises outnumber the weeds, on the order of eight or nine to one.

Cleaning up the weeds is an easy enough job, but handling the surprises is usually a tougher task. I, for example, am hunting for the true identity of a batch of astilbes that I bought last May without much thought and without getting their name. When they finally settled in the garden, their bloom and foliage were not at all what I expected. In time I will get to know them, name or no name, but I think it's impossible to get on well with a plant when you don't know its name.

In any event, I am also filled with questions about birches. Is there a birch tree, I wonder, that will fit my needs or, more precisely, those of my yard? I am looking for a lesson on mountain laurels, too—which ones might fill an opening in the backyard that presently affords porch dwellers a surprisingly rude view of a chain-link fence and the neighbors' brush pile beyond.

These questions are not that difficult to answer, given a little time, and July is for many gardeners just such a time. As gardens reach their peak, their owners enjoy a brief interlude while the plants take care of themselves and the weeds take a short vacation, leaving little to be done. All too soon this interim ends, and suddenly there is a backlog of jobs: deadheading, dividing, transplanting, readying fall orders. But for the moment July allows a respite.

The owner of a new garden probably ought to spend his first year with his hands tied behind his back and his tools locked away in the cellar. The savings in plants and time would be remarkable. Gardeners know this, but if not restrained they forget all good sense at the sight of new soil.

We arrived at our house in the end of December, and I immediately began poking around the yard, examining the shrubs, tugging at the climbing roses. In the months that followed, whenever the snow drew back its cover I prowled about for signs of other plants. Watching the sun, I reckoned its course for the summer and speculated on the chance that sunlight would reach this or that spot. When spring came we turned over various new beds. Occasionally, clumps of root bobbed to the surface, and with little thought for anything but our plans, we discarded them, including a vigorous hollyhock that now needs to be replaced.

Despite all this digging, a number of survivors struggled up as the soil warmed. Bulbs of every sort appeared in every conceivable location. A supposedly dead rose revived and soon overshadowed a dicentra I had planted at its side as a replacement. A peony appeared one day in the bed outside the dining room. Putting out just a few shoots at first, it grew immense before long and toward the end of May opened the first of its twenty-odd blooms, large white affairs with red flecking and the heavy rose fragrance that marked it as 'Festiva Maxima'.

There were surprises where we didn't dig as well. A ratty patch of pachysandra gave way to a large stand of daylilies, which were just what we had in mind for that spot once we got rid of the pachysandra. Nearby, an aging tree lilac in poor health and a poor position seemed a true candidate for the pruning saw. Happily, we spent our time on some other project and so had a chance to enjoy the light, airy flower clusters that covered its branches, more than enough reason for leaving such a tree.

That is not to say everything in the garden belonged there. I was happy to see one mock orange make its way to the shredder, along with many yards of English ivy that had all but strangled a handsome little shrub border. And I still think the neighborhood cats don't belong in my garden, though the cats and I disagree on this. They feel strongly that they deserve a place there, usually on top of a campanula. Like all the other strangers that popped up around the yard, they appeared when the soil had warmed to the temperature of a down comforter. It was clear from the start that, unlike the others, they belonged elsewhere, and I spent a good part of the spring trying to discourage their visits with fits of stomping, waving, and clapping. I'm sure this amused the neighbors, who couldn't see the cats. No doubt it humored the cats, too. All the same, it kept the cats on the move, which is reason enough not to have your hands shackled when you take on a new garden. It's never clear what will show up come spring.

My garden lacks any real sculpture such as you see in most proper gardens. That is not by choice; I am constantly on the lookout for the right piece to stand at the end of a little walk, thereby giving purpose to a path that actually leads to nowhere except a view of the compost pile. However, as yet I've seen nothing that is either acceptable or affordable. Until some other ornament turns up, the spot is ably anchored by a massive, slightly out-of-round terra-rossa pot with pale-orange impatiens spilling over its rim.

Through endless and frivolous spending I am the owner of a large assortment of clay pots. As a group, they constitute the ceramic version of a rogues' gallery. Some are tall with broad shoulders; others are squat and paunchy. Most are quite plainly dressed, though a number are festooned with garlands of some sort. All are ruddy-cheeked, even grimy, showing the scars of hard living, which is how I prefer them. A pot looks best when it's dappled with patches of moss and streaked with dirt.

At the moment they are all brimming with plants, many of them in flower, others on the verge. At the end of April I filled them with annuals and bulbs and set them out on steps, at doorways, and in various other nooks that wanted the help of some pottery and flowers. Eight salmon-colored ivy geraniums flank the four steps to the front door, while a selection of white hybrids gives definition to a set of bland steps up to a deck out back. Nearby, a collection of lilies—'Enchantment', 'Imperial Silver', and a grab bag of anonymous naturalizing lilies—cluster together at the corner of a small terrace. Their lanky height is a welcome addition in such flat, lifeless surroundings. Whether the colors will war with one another is anyone's guess. But whatever the outcome, I imagine they will be a treat seen against the gray paving of the terrace.

Gertrude Jekyll wrote that "where a garden scheme extends over several acres a designer can afford to be severely simple in the details of his conception. . . . A little garden, however, if too simply treated, soon exhausts our curiosity. The more the designer lacks space, the more apt should he be in making us forget his garden's limitations. Ingenious pleasantries of treatment here and there arrest the interest. By concentrating it they make the visitor oblivious to the smallness of the theater which yields so much diversion." While it would certainly stretch the truth to describe my garden as a theater (except for occasional moments of comedy), there is no doubt that the ornamental pots assembled about the place add an element of delightful diversion.

The memory of an elephant is nothing compared to that of a garden hose. Five years ago I bought a heavy-duty hose that is largely if not entirely made of rubber. To this day it retains every original curl and bend. If you coil it according to its particular twists it settles peacefully in its storage place beside a 'Betty Prior' rose. However, in the hands of an unsuspecting person it puts up an awful fight, twisting and twining itself into a tangle that can be undone only by slowly unrolling the entire hose across the lawn and starting again—this time according to the hose's wishes. Even when stretched out it doesn't really lie flat or hold a straight line. It looks more like a snake passing over a series of invisible logs, for every so often it bumps up into the air. The personality of this hose adds an element of danger to the otherwise mundane task of watering because if you fail to pay attention while you go about the yard, the hose will wrap itself around your leg or that of a chair or the base of a large and favorite pot of lilies. Shortly there will be a crash and cursing, and something or someone will need righting.

We eliminated a large portion of the hand-watering that normally goes on around here. The solution, surprisingly, is another hose. This hose is a strange creature, for it does the one thing no one wants a hose to do: It leaks. Made from reconstituted tires, this black hose is better behaved than our normal hose. I unwound it and sank it in the ground throughout our gardens without a struggle. Unlike a canvas soaker hose, which works only when it's laid in a straight line (and then only with limited success), this new one makes U-turns. You could run it along through your radish patch, then turn around and head back through the lettuce crop. In one corner of our yard it loops through some hollies and rhododendrons, then winds among astilbes and hostas.

This new watering method is very efficient, of course, much superior to a hose and nozzle or sprinkler. But it doesn't offer much fun. Everything goes on underground. A sprinkler, on the other hand, is a delight to watch and a pleasure to hear, swaying back and forth, accompanied by the steady patter of water dripping from the well-drenched leaves of trees and shrubs. With the soaker hose buried beneath the soil there is little or no sign of accomplishment, though there is a satisfied feeling that comes with the mixture of efficiency and technology. With a sprinkler, you can see the results. True, you end up watering a good portion of your walk or house (or the neighbor's house, for that matter) and you can count on snapping the flower stalk of a prize delphinium when the flowers fill with water. Your roses are bound to catch a good case of mildew or black spot too. No matter, the lawn glistens; weary and tattered plants pull themselves up out of the dust; bees hover around quenching their thirsts; even the air feels cooler.

The best, most enjoyable method for watering, of course, is a good, drenching downpour. A proper rainstorm, one with all the fixings, adds more than just water to the garden. There is thunder and lightning, usually a wind slashing through the trees; often there's a rainbow off somewhere on the horizon. It may not be the most efficient or effective way to water, but I'll still take a good summer storm over my oscillating sprinkler any day.

Different people weed for different reasons. One woman I know who weeded for money spent her days tackling such jobs as twelve three-hundred-foot-long rows of soybeans, while another woman looking for an education was set to work in a Japanese temple garden removing single strands of emerging grass from a moss bed.

We have weeds of all sorts in all places. They begin out on the sidewalk, where all manner of sturdy tramps survive drought, scorching sun, occasional applications of salt during the winter, and the constant battering of pedestrians (and their dogs) through the summer. There are pigweeds and plantains, knotweeds and ailanthus seedlings. These weeds are only a foot or two from a thin strip of garden that is filled with peonies, clematises, climbing roses, and a number of other worthy plants. Only a wall of wooden fencing separates the weeds in the walk from the plants in the garden. So although it would be easiest to blanket the walk with some herbicide, I spray rarely and nervously. I don't want to rid the sidewalk of every plant; there is something reassuring about tufts of green sprouting between the bricks.

Most of the weeds in our yard live in the lawn—chickweed, crabgrass, dandelions, plantains, purslane, and the like. I have turned my back on them so far; they make up less than 25 percent of the lawn, and so, according to the late Jim Crockett, there's no need to dig it up.

The weeds that worry me most are not the oxalis or the wild

onions or any of the other well-known interlopers. Our garden is small, and such weeds are never so numerous that I can't control them during my regular rounds. They give me something to do during this period of the year when there's nothing else that demands my attention. The most troubling weeds are those plants that I want in my garden but not by the thousands. I am blessed with countless corydalises; I find malvas popping up all over; the geraniums are the most rampant and tenacious (though a single Norway maple is equal match for any number of them). Yet in some spots these upstarts fit the bill perfectly, and I wouldn't want them all taken away even if it were possible. Every time I come across a stray seedling, I have to decide whether it would actually improve the garden—which is largely a shade garden, after all. If not, should I move the seedling somewhere else? Or pot it up and offer it to a friend who admired it? (This raises the question of whether you should give a friend a plant you know will overrun him.)

It's difficult to weed too slowly though easy to go too fast. If you rush to clean an entire bed—peas or peonies—of anything, you will end up nicking plants you set out to nurture. You will also miss the first signs of an aphid infestation or an outbreak of rust. There is very little in gardening that benefits from being done quickly, and weeding teaches the virtues of pace as well as any activity.

I dream of a garden acres across, with a stream flowing through one corner and plenty of sunlight. The garden I inhabit, however, is a fraction of an acre. The only water comes from two faucets, which the water department says I can open only between the hours of 8 P.M. and 7 A.M. There is shade everywhere you look.

In the winter, when the nursery catalogs arrive, I pick and choose plants happily, without regard to their size, their need for full sun, or their ability to go without water. I never send these orders, of course; my garden has neither the conditions nor the shoulder room for a *Crambe cordifolia* or a *Rheum palmatum*. A single plant of either would span it in places.

One of the advantages of a small garden is that it forces you to concentrate and be creative. There is no room for plants that make a great show once a year and spend the rest of their time lounging in a ratty housecoat. In a large garden you might devote a bed to peonies or poppies or asters. With less space you need plants that contribute after their moment of glory is past.

Bulbs such as lilies and alliums extend and enhance the life of my small kingdom. On their own, neither comes to mind as particularly valuable. Both are spindly plants with unexciting foliage. But both share the trait of happily growing up through the foliage of other plants. The benefits of this arrangement are numerous. The gawky posture of these tall bulb plants is diminished because a third or so of each stem is hidden by another plant's more attractive foliage. The underplanting meanwhile gains an appearance of height. In my garden lilies emerge from clumps of epimediums, geraniums, hostas, and astilbes. The thin wispy stems of the alliums look less skimpy sprouting out of a stand of handsome tiarellas in one spot and from among some hemerocallis in another. Elsewhere a lone specimen of *Hosta* 'Frances Williams' stands majestic above a carpet of English ivy. This sort of idea is not a new one; inventive gardeners have practiced such tricks for a long time, building tiered plantings that rise in succession through the season. I wonder how there can be enough room underground for all the roots.

The English have refined this technique to an art form in their container plantings. Some tallish plant, either upright by nature or trained as a standard, will be surrounded and supported by a variety of annuals and perennials, some standing at a lesser height, others spilling over the pot's edge. These lush and nicely shaggy pyramids are entire gardens in themselves. I have tried my hand at this, but my efforts so far have an awkward appearance. Rather than mingling harmoniously, the plants in my containers give the impression that they don't quite trust each other. It reminds me of the atmosphere at a high-school dance, the uncomfortable clusters of boys and girls dotting the floor at safe distances from one another.

Planted in containers or otherwise, bulbs lend themselves to this many-tiered style. They are content with a modest amount of space underground in return for which they make an extravagant display. No need to worry that your garden is filling up, that you must either move or yank something out. There is always extra space hiding in your garden.

With the world three-quarters covered in water, there ought to be enough to go around. In the Northeast it often seems there is more than enough. This spring, especially, it appeared that any time I looked with interest at the garden, clouds would move in quickly and snuff out my intentions with a downpour. Some of the best weekends were rained out start to finish. In the end I planted in the rains and mowed between them. The lawn didn't rest for a minute from April on, and by the end of May I had cut hundreds of inches of grass. But as always happens, we will need more water before the summer is out. Everyone in this part of the country expects to run short on rain in July and August, and we grouse about lugging hoses around and setting up sprinklers. We curse the bright, clear days and pray for a sky thick with oily rain clouds.

While gardeners in the Northeast worry about a lack of rain in August, people in many other parts of the country think about a lack of water on a daily basis. This worry colors the activities of any gardener west of the Rockies. Call and ask friends in California how the water situation stands and they will give you a detailed account. They know the amount of rain that fell in the last six months and how it compares to the annual averages. They can tell you the state of the snowpack in the Sierras and how much water the runoff will contribute to the area. You can get a rundown on the levels of important reservoirs. People in California follow water rates the way New Yorkers study the Dow Jones averages.

The news on the western water front is rarely cheering. While we in the East get 20 inches or more of rainfall from May through October (Boston receives 19.57; Miami, 43.89), people in the far West can count on 10 inches (Seattle, 10.42;

Portland, 9.8) or much less (San Francisco, 1.95; Los Angeles, 0.86). A lawn grass needs roughly 12 inches of water during these months.

In Santa Barbara, California, a city known for its lush landscapes, the local government confronted the problem head on a couple of years ago by instituting a law that banned watering lawns with sprinklers. Violators can be fined, and repeat offenders can have their water shut off. Water rates were increased eightfold. (People addicted to lawns can choose to have their grass spray-painted green.) The city is encouraging homeowners to switch to drip-irrigation systems; there is also serious interest in gray water, water that is not drinkable but can be recycled for use on plants. The concept may not sound appealing, but in Santa Barbara, such alternatives make the distasteful facts easier to swallow.

We must all learn from California's lessons. We are exhausting our water supplies plain and simple, and the day is not far off when every gardener will know the intimacies of drip emitters, soaker hoses, and drought-tolerant plants, and the glories of groundcovers and mulches. These ideas are not new, just not widely circulated. Technology exists to get water to plants economically. The lawn grass industry has been developing grasses that withstand heat and drought without going entirely to pieces. There is no end to the possibilities for wonderful and exciting gardens. But there is certainly an end to the water, no matter how things look in May.

A garden in the early morning is a magical land, full of ornate cobwebs sagging with dew, soft shadows, and the eager chatter of birds going on about the current crop of worms and the shiftiness of squirrels. Birds and squirrels and worms are up early at this time of year, and so are many gardeners. They all have work to do, and the prospect of toiling under the midday sun is disagreeable. This mood suits the work that needs doing—many gardens have now taken on a tattered, bedraggled appearance. Some of this look is natural enough; certainly in the vegetable garden a look of fruitful weariness is no surprise. But in the ornamental borders the disarray often reflects the exhaustion of the gardener more than that of the plants. There is a constant supply of tasks, but they demand neither great strength nor speed. Instead what the gardener needs is a sharp eye and a steady hand.

I begin most mornings in the garden with a haze in my eyes and a mug of coffee in my hands. Occasionally I have a job in mind and go right to it. But more often I make a circuit, looking for plants that need attention and deciding where to start. I also try to enjoy the good spots, catching the fragrance of *Calamintha nepeta*, which spills onto the path and gushes a scent of mint as I brush past it, or watching the bumblebees scavenge the flowers of the Russian sage, the buddleias, the clethras. The bees' journeys appear random and their work erratic. But in a deliberate and determined fashion they get the job done, and their methods suit me admirably in high summer.

I keep our wheelbarrow filled with an assortment of bamboo

poles, twine, pruning shears, and a favorite hand hoe. By making regular rounds with these tools—combing weeds and dead flowers from the beds, reviving exhausted plants with food and drink, and propping up some with a cane or two, I keep the beds alive and interesting. It is methodical work, requiring precision and persistence. Getting into the crowded beds involves a leap of faith (faith that you aren't going to crush a desirable hellebore seedling), combined with the ability to freeze my body with one foot wedged between a daylily and a monarda and the other curled around a stand of geraniums. Settled in this manner I pull weeds and cut dead flowers, bending this way and that so as to reach the last blossom without plunging facefirst into the nearby *Rosa* 'Königin von Dänemark'. It ends up resembling a solo performance of some modern dance—another good reason for tackling the work early in the day, when fewer people are likely to see you. When there's nothing left to do within reach, I gingerly retreat. As in so many of life's activities, extracting yourself is often more difficult than getting in at the start.

I pause regularly to rest my back, to check on progress, and to finish off the lukewarm coffee, assuming the ants haven't discovered it. In this fashion the work proceeds slowly, but the wheelbarrow fills surprisingly fast with weeds and spent flowers. The work in the late-summer garden is slow, often repetitive, and without the grand gestures of the spring planting extravaganza. But it offers sure proof that the garden is growing and that there are pleasures, sometimes small but still rewarding, to be gained in the process.

AUGUST

AMONG THE PLANTS THAT I KNOW, I CANNOT THINK OF one that does not make a good cut flower. Certain of the peonies last only a short while, some of the climbing roses and the astilbes lack enough stem for my intentions (which we will get to in a bit), and there are others for which I simply lack a suitable container. Such complaints are small, though, compared to the pleasure—different with every bloom—that these flowers offer.

Ours is not a cutting garden in the sense of a plot laid out and planted solely for the purpose of filling vases every day. Ours is, rather, a garden in which no plant is immune to occasional cutting, and over time we have come to a greater appreciation of certain plants through this policy. The first of these was heuchera. For a time I dismissed its rosy sprays, but having brought them indoors I began to fully appreciate their finely cut edges, tall, sturdy stems, and the longevity of their blooms. Even a few stems add a delicate air to gatherings of taller flowers, but they appeal to me as well set against the foliage of blue-gray hosta leaves and nothing else. I like lavender for some of the same reasons. Its flowers are not as handsome as heuchera's perhaps, but their color is strong and clear. Dotted here and there among other more grand trumpeters like lilies, they contribute a fine accent despite their small stature. That is not a slight against lilies, though; once cut and brought inside they lose any awkwardness they might display in the garden and gain an elegance that is hard to match.

Shrubs also take their place in our cutting garden. They lengthen its season at both ends, and some of them bolster the meek personalities of less fortunate flowers. The forsythia and lilac are best known for this talent, and many people overlook their shortcomings in favor of their merits as cut flowers. There are many other excellent shrubs that warrant the attention of our shears. Potentillas are a particularly fine example, if only for their delicate foliage, which complements late daffodils and tulips. And I also like the red-leaved shrubs, such as berberis, as accents for cut flowers.

It should be clear that I worry little about the formal rules of arranging cut flowers. My arrangements (that is really too grand a word for what I do) suffer for this carefree attitude, no doubt, but I compose them for my own satisfaction (and my wife's, I hope), and friends who visit are free to laugh. The flowers usually make the best of my unguided enthusiasm.

The best time to travel is whenever you find the chance. Any month will do. You can always find places and plants that will suit your fancy—and some that don't, which is just as valuable. The same garden visited at different seasons will show entirely different faces and moods, teaching new lessons and providing new delights. There is no chance of ever coming to know a garden with one visit. The people who tend them are always adding plants they've never grown and chucking out ones they've tired of. Not long ago, for example, I went to see Stonecrop, Frank Cabot's garden in Cold Spring, New York. It is a large garden made of numerous small rooms. What was most interesting were the great many changes Frank and his associate Caroline Burgess had made and are continuing to make. Where there had been strictly perennials, now there are also annuals. The vegetable garden has changed in size and shape. There was talk about changing grass walks to paving. In short, the garden is expanding at every turn as new plants and new planting ideas are introduced. (That may be a drawback of having someone helping you in a garden—one more head full of projects.) With all these alterations newly under way, the garden lacked some of the fullness that will come in a year or so, but it showed the vitality of a garden where people are hard at work.

Often there is no time to get away during the spring and

early summer, the season when many gardens look their best. Come August both gardens and gardeners are often worn and weary. But there can easily be more in the garden now than a hammock filled with a sleeping gardener. Many plants show their best at this season: perennials such lobelias, monardas, echinops; shrubs such as clethras and buddleias, to name but a few. You may come across late-blooming varieties of plants you know well—daylilies, salvias, or thalictrums, for instance—along with those that will happily throw a second flush of bloom if you cut them back after their spring display. The unique qualities that water brings to a garden—reflecting the occasional cloud, conjuring up the sound of a refreshing stream—are especially welcome in the torrid days of midsummer. Likewise the admirable tenacity of annuals, blooming endlessly despite dry and fiery conditions. The richly colored elegance of lilies (to say nothing of their fragrance), the cooling blues of aconitums, the cascade of a *Clematis maximowicziana* in full flower and thick with its honeylike scent—all these plants give their best at high summer. At seed houses and all-American testing sites, trial gardens are reaching their peak. Great clumps of tomatoes hang from the vines, and long rows of annuals gush with color. If you have never liked marigolds, you are sure to here.

No matter what the time of year or the glad tidings of the weatherman, take rubber boots of some sort when you go visiting, and probably an umbrella, too. It may not rain, but if you go early in the morning—the best time to see a garden—the ground will be soaking and you will be spending more time listening to the *shrunch* of your socks than admiring the climbing roses you came especially to see. But should you forget the boots and the umbrella, don't worry; there's usually enough sun to dry you out a this time of year.

When I was growing up, I shared with my brother the duty of putting our dog out in her kennel each night. Although it required a trip of fifty feet or less, I dreaded those outings. I knew that once I closed the latch on the dog's pen and turned back to the house, all sorts of ghouls and goblins—not to mention escaped lunatics and criminals—lurked behind the lilacs with the goal of tearing me limb from limb. It was a race through the dark to the house. I always ran, and I always arrived breathless. The idea of going out into that world to look at the garden never crossed my mind. In the city, however, the night is never so dark or so scary, and the garden often looks, smells, and sounds best after dark.

Our night garden begins to unfold well before dark, in the hour before sunset. The shadows are long, and the rough edges of the garden—worn spots in the lawn, browned leaf tips of iris—begin to disappear. Only a few rays of sunlight find their way in, and only the glossiest leaves, like those of bergenia and asarum, can hold them. Long after dark these plants glow with remnants of the day's light.

When the bergenias and asarums finally recede into the darkness, other plants take their place in lighting the garden. In early summer the dense clusters of white and yellow climbing roses are most noticeable. Against the gray-blue shingles of the house, they seem suspended in air like so many distant constellations; likewise the furry double flowers of *Clematis* 'Duchess of Edinburgh'. Down on the ground, galaxies of white flowers mark the boundaries of various beds: the nodding white bells of *Hosta* 'Frances Williams'; a clump of almost pure-white shasta daisies; *Geranium sanguineum* 'Album'; *Lilium* 'Sterling Star', with its simple, graceful flowers; and a trio of oakleaf hydrangeas whose trusses of white blossoms look like eyes peeking out beneath the bush eyebrows of overarching hemlocks.

You can see all these plants from the safety of our terrace, but if you prowl around the yard you will encounter other plants that are still active in the night. Creamy-flowered foxgloves hide among the foliage of daylilies, *Euonymus* 'Emerald 'n' Gold' shimmers beneath a viburnum, and *Hosta* 'Piedmont Gold' glows in a shady corner. Although you won't see its deep-blue flower spikes, you might brush against a stand of lavender and catch a breath of its heavy scent. At the right time of year you can't avoid the potent perfume of peony 'Festiva Maxima' or the yellow rose 'Doubloons' along the front fence. With a slight wind from the right direction you'll pick up the lemon scent of lilies unseen at the back of a bed.

Tying all this together is the darkness. It too changes throughout the garden, from a dusky quality near the house to pitch black beneath the hemlocks. The night's varied shades change the character of the garden, erasing both its flaws and, in the deepest shadows, its boundaries. Our garden has one personality by day, another by night. I am thankful for the night garden, but I like to keep the lights of home in sight.

With the possible exception of squirrels, gardeners may be the most acquisitive creatures on earth. Even well-balanced gardeners order a good number of seeds each year "just to try," and few can leave a nursery without buying at least three items they did not need. Led on by catalogs, books, and the stories of friends, they will pursue a good plant for years.

Some gardeners lose their hearts to one plant. If it is hostas they fancy, they will grow all the kinds that garden and checkbook allow and will not sleep soundly if a shipment of new hybrids is due from Japan. Other gardeners focus their attention on plants from a particular country and are not content until they have grown or at least seen everything from, say, China. They will save up vacation time and money, then desert family and friends to spend three weeks overseas gathering choice plants, in the meantime collecting rare forms of dysentery and tapeworm as well.

I recently made a brief trip around England with two friends who like plants of all colors and denominations. Their appetite is insatiable, and they have worked their collection into a wonderful garden in Vermont. When we decided last winter to make the trip, my friends calmly announced that they intended to bring plants home. This is something I have never attempted myself, for I lacked the nerve or patience to tackle the labyrinthian bureaucracy that deals out permits, to say nothing of the likelihood of the plants dying slow and grue-some deaths in a customs warehouse somewhere. None of this deterred my companions, who arrived in England with a bulging packet of permits. By the end of the first day the trunk of our rental car was half full of plants, and before long both the trunk and rear seat resembled small gardens. I especially liked the placement of a large-leaved rhubarb next to a lightly variegated spirea.

Before we could send the plants home, we had to wash them and get them inspected. Like miners panning for gold, we care-fully teased out every grain of soil from the root balls. Inspec-tors came and scrutinized the plants, which were naked but for a skimpy coating of peat moss. We then packed our certified-sanitary plants in two unassuming boxes and left them on a British Airways loading dock. We departed with a mixture of elation and sadness, the sort of feeling a parent has watching a child go off for the first day of school.

The plants reached their final destination one week later, after stopping in New York to overcome jet lag and the suspi-cions of more plant inspectors. All in all, the process required nearly fifty phone calls, four or five faxes, numerous letters, three boxes of plastic bags, and great quantities of time and money. But not only were the plants alive when they arrived, they looked like they had enough energy left to turn around and make the trip again. That seems a small price to pay for a few wonderful additions to the garden.

Gardeners are among that class of people who raise puttering to the state of high art. Their activities in midsummer constitute an endless round of small chores that to them possess levels of purpose but to passersby must appear like the actions of a slightly distracted uncle stopping now and then to stoop and paw at the soil. There is erratic traffic with watering cans, disappearances into the toolshed. And always the gardener is apt to stop in midstride and plunge into the garden to right some plant or some less well defined wrong. The impression is of someone who has lost something and doesn't know where to look for it.

In fact, they are looking for something. They are looking for trouble—for outbreaks of plague or pestilence, for hints of hunger or thirst, for signs of aggression. They are also on alert for more promising notes—unexpected or forgotten seedlings, renewed vigor in a sulking plant, signals that this or that plant will send forth another round of flowers. In my own garden so many things need watching that I find I need to get up with the sun to accomplish even a small portion of the work.

This summer, in addition to the normal weeding, watering, deadheading, pruning, and trimming, I have been tending a pile of mulch. Thanks to a neighbor whose appetite for mulch was bigger than his garden's needs, I came into five cubic yards of pine bark. Dumped in front of our garage, it made a pile slightly higher than the hood of our Volkswagen and perhaps three-quarters as long as the car itself. Not much, but it took me nearly a month to spread it about the garden. Putting down mulch in midsummer means putting it down by the handful.

You have to tuck it in under the wide spreading leaves of mulleins, crambes, bergenias, and geraniums; toss it delicately beneath Scotch thistles, junipers, roses, and mahonias; and sift it softly among stands of irises and astilbe. For most of June and early July, I kept a loaded wheelbarrow by my side. When I didn't have anything else to do I put down mulch.

Much of the rest of the time I was taking up weeds. The silver maple that overhangs one section of the garden sent down a huge crop of seeds, scattering them a good distance throughout the garden. They emerged in great numbers and in every possible location—beneath the broad skirts of hostas and viburnums, deep in the middle of dense clumps of sedums and daylilies. They came out easily with a tug, but the sheer numbers kept me busy for a month. What with cleaning up spring bulb plantings and deadheading early summer blooms, I managed to take nearly as many loads to the compost pile as I brought in from the mulch pile. There is a satisfying symmetry to the equation.

The beauty of jobs that go slowly and are done at ground level is that you get to know your plants in a way that just isn't possible from the seat of a speeding lawn mower. In the rush of spring's endless jobs it is hard to notice the plants. In the slower pace of summer there is a chance to watch the garden unfold, to notice troubles, and to appreciate small details.

At this time of the year my day begins and ends with the watering of pots. It is the one constant. Pots are scattered around the house and garden, requiring numerous trips to and from the faucet. The slow pace forced by carrying a two-gallon can and the repetitiveness of my route gives me time to study the garden and plan the fall planting season. The work nicely suits either end of the day. In the early evening I attend those pots I didn't get to in the morning, and if the day was warm I am able to dip the can into our children's wading pool.

The pots in our garden have increased over time, like any interest that holds your attention. Stood side by side, they make the gardening equivalent of a police lineup. There are large and small pots, many that are plain, others that are slightly ornamented with garlands or handles. All of them show signs of life. The ones that are used every year wear the green-and-white grizzle that comes from sleeping out over time. A good number bear the scars, small nicks, or cracks that are unavoidable in a long life. Each year we add a few members to this motley collection. And inevitably we lose a few to old age or mishandling, or to friends who take them away with some plant.

The life these pots lead in our garden is as informal as the pots themselves. Three or four spend their summers right in the borders, placed on old bricks and nestled among perennials and low shrubs. A bulbous-shaped one sits on the stump of a Norway maple. For the last two years it has held the black-and-white salvia (*S. discolor*), whose simple but striking looks add a bit of life to an otherwise quiet stretch of planting. In the center of the vegetable garden four pots filled with herbs surround a standard bay. Together they lend a look of order to the vegetables, which are especially disheveled at this time of year.

Elsewhere, pots cover a multitude of blemishes. A small cluster hides a barren patch near the garage door, others hide the rough edges of some fieldstone steps I constructed; still others fill the awkward nooks on either side of the bulkhead.

Almost anything can be grown in a pot. From hefty trees and shrubs to delicate bulbs, plants prosper in containers. Hostas shine in a manner impossible when planted in a mass. The same is true of cannas and, I suspect, of grasses. A friend has convinced me that the only way to achieve showlike perfection with delphiniums is to grow them singly in pots where they can indulge their appetite for eating and drinking, then return to obscurity once they pass their prime.

The popular style of planting pots these days is to sneak in as many plants as possible. The goal is to achieve something between a jungle and a Jekyllian border in a twenty-inch container. Some plants are trained upward, others allowed to sprawl, the rest to mingle happily. If they are well planted, such pots are glorious concoctions, intricate and thrilling jumbles. Because my efforts generally result in plantings that are more tangled than thrilling, I prefer to grow one type of plant in each pot. Nothing looks as fresh on a hot day as a neat ball of boxwood or an arching spray of nicotiana. They are at ease whether the setting is casual or formal. Many pots, especially those of great stature or pure simplicity, look as good filled with nothing. The value of having pots in a garden goes beyond the beauty of the pots or the flowers that fill them.

Just when to harvest a vegetable is a matter of deep and divisive debate among gardeners. Indeed, there are probably as many methods for judging ripeness as there are gardeners. The thumpers, for example, are a well-known group whose many advocates go around whacking all their vegetables, listening for the certain timbre that signals perfect ripeness. (They disagree, however, about the proper technique for thumping; some favor the open palm, others insist on the merits of a closed fist.) Another crowd holds the theory that certain crops will drop from their vines when mature, while some gardeners watch the color of their plants, looking for the perfect yellow or green. Others follow the schedules printed on the seed packets. I prefer to take a bite of whatever I'm harvesting—I plan to eat the stuff, not turn it into a drum.

No matter what theory you follow, the tools for harvesting are few in number and simple in technology. It is true that the people who make money selling tools have concocted some specialized and even complicated devices, impossible as that may seem. But they are hard put to improve on a gardener's two natural tools, his hands. Add to them a basket of some sort and an old kitchen knife, and the outfit is complete for most purposes. Actually that is only true until the garden hits its stride and three or four crops need harvesting all at once. Then most people need a fleet of wheelbarrows. This is the time when gardeners wail that next year they will pay attention to the timing instructions, so as to avoid this crush. And they promise themselves—and anyone else within listening distance—that they will plant only half as much of everything.

(Really, a quarter would be more sensible.) Nonetheless, year after year, they are left with a harvest that would bust anyone's cornucopia.

It is a commandment among gardeners that even if you planted enough Brussels sprouts to feed the entire neighborhood, Thou shalt not throw away a single sprout. This code is observed with such determination that countless children have forever lost their appetites for this or that vegetable after eating it nonstop for three weeks, and it has caused well-meaning cooks to devise some of the most bizarre recipes imaginable—beet-and-zucchini pancakes, for instance, or rhubarb fritters.

At some point either your digestive tract or your family relations break down under the relentless repetition of such menus, and you must turn to some manner of preserving the remainder of your crops. I realize many people will disagree with me, but I think the only sound argument for preserving food is an economic one, and I suspect that if you accounted for all the costs involved, this argument would fall apart. However, forgetting taste and excepting fruits like strawberries and raspberries, which are almost improved by a stay in the freezer, by the middle of March one package of frozen beans tastes pretty much like any other, which is to say not great.

Luckily, by the middle of March gardeners generally aren't thinking much about their taste buds. Their thoughts are on the season ahead, the weather it holds in store, and the prospect, beginning about this time, of a bountiful harvest.

Irrigation is efficient and dependable, and rain is neither, but there are few events that can match a summer rainstorm for direct and dramatic pleasure. Even a brief afternoon shower magically stirs all five senses. A summer downpour is one of those delights, like letters from friends, that are wonderful partly because they come irregularly, often when you least expect them, and sometimes when you need them most.

Each rainfall is different, with a look and sound of its own, making up a cast of characters equal to nature's stage. There are gentle, almost shy rains. They often appear at night, barely rustling the tree leaves, dispensing their gifts and disappearing by morning. Some rains are sulking and miserly, never quite raining but never quite finished. Other times the play of light and water gives an almost comical quality to the scene. The opposite character appears in the thunder and lightning storms of hot, high summer days. These raucous storms shut out the light. Their downpour is near deafening. In their wake the ground is often covered with leaves and torn branches; the garden borders lie battered as though a madman has gone on a rampage.

If the rain is not too fierce or accompanied by lightning, I like to go into the garden, either to work or to wander around. It is a good time for planting seedlings and for pulling weeds, of course. Slugs come out to lounge on the stones of the path, as do earthworms—you need to watch your step, or you can be sure to squash the one and avoid the other. In a hard rain some plants may need help standing up, and I often find I am like a gardener's Red Cross, ferrying pea brush and linking stakes to beleaguered plants. More often, however, the plants are able to withstand the falling rain and even flourish in it. Sun-wary plants suddenly rise up, their spirits rejuvenated by the storm. Even those that are bent seem to have a grace that is rare in a plant covered in snow: The rain-soaked shrub has the graceful curve of a dancer, while the same shrub in winter has the crooked look of an exhausted laborer. Often I huddle beneath the branches of a spreading dogwood tree or the overhanging eaves of the toolshed to watch and listen as the rain beats down and the thirsty ground soaks up the moisture.

Other than in the garden, the next best place to be during a rain is on a porch. When I was growing up, our family would often gather on the back porch to review a storm as it marched across the lawn and garden, swept over the hay fields beyond, and climbed into the mountains in the distance. Storm watching was a particular favorite of my father's when there was lightning. Then we would try to guess the distance of the flashes by counting "one-one thousand, two-one thousand," and so on in the interval between the flash and the thunder. My father relished the activity; I, however, didn't, fearing electrocution at any time. I spent the moments between flashes trying to fashion an argument that would convince him of the sense of installing lightning rods.

Eventually, the tumultuous, tumbling torrents of high summer give way to autumn's cool and gentle soakings, reflecting the season as do the delicate rains of early spring and the long soakings of early summer. The water is always welcome, no less so than the sounds and the scents that accompany every rainfall.

To some gardeners the best news about August is that it eventually turns into September. In August the lawn suffers from heat stroke, powdery mildew tortures the monarda, and the pieris is a meal for spider mites. There are bright spots, of course, and if you are a vegetable gardener there is much to cheer about—a bounty of corn and cukes, the prospect of broccoli and pumpkins and fall crops to follow. But our yard is not so large as to allow a vegetable garden of any size, so such good news is largely lost on me. Without a watering system or melons on the vine, come August, I am listless and withering like most of my plants.

The oasis in these dry and dusty days is the fall catalog. It is true that many if not all of them arrive in early July, but there is plenty to do in the garden at that point and even more to admire, so they wait in a pile on the kitchen counter. The catalogs of fall promise a bright future quite unlike that of the spring listings. The fall catalogs are smaller, but they contain a range of plants certain to succeed, a relief to gardeners convinced that their climates are not fit for anything except maybe a few succulents. In January the catalogs are different in character, and so are the gardeners. With fall behind them and winter all around, they are easy prey to the attractions of this or that plant. But the fall catalog finds gardeners low on hope and thin on patience, unsure of their abilities. The dog days of summer are under way, and a gardener is not easily persuaded by the large and colorful photographs of phlox standing tall with full heads of bloom. Out the window he can see his own phlox crippled by mildew (except occasionally 'Miss Lingard', a remarkably healthy cultivar), looking more like a candidate for a bread line than a garden aristocrat. He counts himself lucky, then, to open the fall catalog and find tulips and narcissi, fritillarias, amaryllises, and loads of lilies. Plus peonies.

Peonies are among the finest plants for a garden. They survive most any conditions, in most any location. Light shade doesn't seem to put them off their good demeanor. Their flowers are richly colored, large, and elegant without appearing pompous or gaudy, as is the case with so many flowers after the hybridizers have been at them for a century. You can find peonies in all shades of red and pink and white. With some luck you can buy them cheaply at an out-of-the-way nursery or get a few tubers from a friend who is not bothered by the myth that they dislike transplanting and won't flower after being moved. The form of the petals varies. Some flowers are single, simple blooms that open wide, while others are ruffled and layered like the feathers of an ostrich (or an eagle if you're not keen on ostriches). Many have yellow stamens, which make a nice contrast to the cleanly colored flowers. When they finish blooming, the plants hold their handsome good looks until the killing frosts, immune to the normal wear and tear of summer. Even in the fall peonies carry a fine bronze foliage. That is the sort of long season—not just two weeks of bloom followed by three months in a nursing home—that a gardener dreams about in August and is happy to contemplate in September.

SEPTEMBER

WITH THE EXCEPTION OF ONE COUPLE LIVING IN SOUTH-
ern New Jersey, everyone is peddling bulbs this year. No salesman has yet come calling at my door, but in every other respect
the activity has been feverish. Well before the first bulbs began
pushing up through the winter mulch outside, I had bulb
offers coming in through the mail slot: catalogs, brochures,
booklets, flyers, even a letter sent by air from Holland. The bill
from one of my credit cards included an offer for tulips along
with pitches for full home-entertainment centers and sets of
designer luggage.

The reason so many people are selling bulbs is simple.
Getting started in business is just about as difficult as setting
up a lemonade stand. You need a few dollars, a Dutchman as a

friend, and the addresses of some gardeners. You don't need a field because you can arrange to have the bulbs sent directly from the grower to the gardener. You might need a computer if business gets going strong.

Choosing to plant bulbs is like choosing to wear a white shirt—you'll almost never go wrong. If you own a formal-looking terrace, say, you can assemble a regiment of tulips to stand at attention like the queen's guard. In the openings of a herbaceous border or along the front of some shrubs you might nestle a few fritillarias, some scilla, or maybe muscari. The possibilities are endless, as they say, and gardeners would do well to study the example of the British, who stop at nothing to wedge a few more plants into a garden and plant bulbs any-where, with anything.

I am not discriminating about bulbs, as you can probably tell. I received some of my bulbs as gifts, bought others as collections, and gratefully inherited a large array of them from the previous owner of our house. Sadly, I cannot identify more than a few, though I like them all and would gladly learn their names. At night I read the bulb catalogs, which form a tall pile beside the bed, though I still doubt I could pick out a named hybrid even with a catalog in my hands.

If I could own just a single bulb, I would choose a daffodil, one such as 'Ice Follies', with sturdy stems, some fragrance, and above all a healthy tendency to increase itself. I might put that one bulb below the viburnum across from the front door, or maybe at the base of the sugar maple, where I could watch its progress from the kitchen. Most likely, though, it would wind up under the dogwood at the end of the walk. Even a single daffodil nodding under a dogwood can conjure up visions of vast woodlands carpeted with spring flowers. That is all I ask of a daffodil, and I've yet to see one that couldn't handle the job.

I'd love to sell bulbs someday, though I know I never will. It's not that the job is more difficult than it seems, which it is. What worries me is the certain truth that I'd manage my bulbs the same way I did my lemonade stand: In a flash I'd have all the bulbs planted around my yard and no money in the till. All the same, it might just be worth it.

Every gardener ought to own at least a small stretch of stone wall, and there is nothing to assembling such an edifice beyond some groaning and the loss of a couple fingernails. Not long after we moved to our house I laid a small wall of fieldstone, some thirty feet long, two feet high, and shaped roughly like a crescent. After it was finished I filled in the slight depression behind it and so ended up with a new bit of garden. Although I had never built one by myself before, this was not my first turn at wall building. When I was younger I occasionally helped my father construct long runs of stone wall. He seemed to be building, rebuilding, or moving a wall every year. He made serious walls involving small tractors, ropes, crowbars, and stone boats. The rocks always came from some part of our property: an old wall, a crumbling barn foundation, a new square of recently turned ground. In a land constantly spitting up rocks, we never wanted for materials.

Finding rocks in the city can take you on a long and frustrating hunt. Some people get lucky and stumble upon a source. A friend of mine, looking to erect a small retaining wall outside his greenhouse, struck a deal with a nearby golf course to haul away rocks from the perimeter of its land. This shortened the life of his car by some years, but he figured another car was easier to come by than a large supply of free rocks. He was right. My five tons of stone cost almost as much as I paid for my first car, and I had to wait three months before they were delivered. I found them easily enough: Suppliers advertise in the yellow pages. (The idea of people selling rocks through the phone book amused my friends in the country.) Many rock dealers offer fieldstone as a sideline to their real business of selling cemetery monuments.

Building walls is a slow and methodical job; there is a right spot for each stone and a right stone for each spot. Some rocks drop into place without the slightest problem; others need to be flipped and spun and juggled and moved here and there before finding a suitable place.

I took four days and fifty-odd wheelbarrow loads to construct the wall, the time divided about evenly between wheeling the rocks across the lawn and pondering their position. With the stones in place I then made arrangements to receive six cubic yards of topsoil, which I dumped in behind the wall. I planted the bed late in the fall, and as a finishing touch this spring I persuaded my father to bring down a few large flat stones for a small sitting area. (He had some extras left over from a wall he'd gotten free from a neighbor.)

The whole project, not including any plants, cost me several hundred dollars. That price does include one pair of thick leather gloves, which started the job new and ended up full of holes. The quality of the construction will not land me in the Masons' Hall of Fame. The thing is gap-toothed in spots, and the batter could be better. All the same I am glad for its presence. It provides a handsome gray backdrop for the plants along its front and a useful stage for those behind. Here and there lichen color the rocks in shades of green. And in the approaching seasons when nothing is growing, the wall will give the garden shape and height and beauty.

The chrysanthemum always enjoys great popularity in Japan. Since A.D. 797, the flower has been the emblem of the emperor, and so it is much in the news. And in September the country holds its annual chrysanthemum festival, a celebration of this flower, which the Japanese believe has the power of long life. In the world of gardening, however, the life is going out of the chrysanthemum. It isn't the flower it used to be.

There is nothing wrong with the plant's vitality. Chrysanthemums brighten the front steps and borders of countless houses each fall, and tantalizing new cultivars are appearing in ever increasing numbers. The trouble has to do with their name. Until recently the genus *Chrysanthemum* contained around two hundred species; then taxonomists began splitting it up into fourteen new genera. When they were done, only three species, all annual herbs from the Mediterranean, remained as true chrysanthemums. About forty species, comprising most of the roughly seven thousand cultivated varieties called "mums," took on the name *Dendranthema*. The well-known Shasta daisy changed its name to *Leucanthemum*, while genera include *Arctanthemum*, *Coleostephus*, *Hymenostemma*, *Leucanthemopsis*, and *Nipponanthemum*. In theory, chrysanthemums all but ceased to exist.

There are two main reasons for all this chopping up and hiving off. The rules for naming plants, as stated by the International Code of Botanical Nomenclature and the International Code of Nomenclature of Cultivated Plants, are extensive, exacting, and still evolving. One of the fundamental laws is that the earliest validly published name of a plant takes precedence. Therefore if someone discovers an older name that has somehow been overlooked, that name takes over. But a greater cause of change has been the advancing sophistication of taxonomy. As one author wrote in *HortScience*, the classifications made in this century have been "based on cytology, embryology, hybridization, and phytochemistry."

All this careful high science makes no difference to many gardeners, who have trouble enough dealing with the Latin name they know and—in the case of chrysanthemums—love. At this year's annual meeting of the British Royal Horticultural Society, one member, a Mr. Philip, took the director and his associates to task over this matter. Mr. Philip complained that "the publication of *The New RHS Dictionary of Gardening* has revealed many hundreds of new and unfamiliar genera, to which familiar and widely available plants have now been relegated. We have now to ask, for example, for *Hylotelephium* 'Autumn Joy', instead of *Sedum*."

Not all the changes made by taxonomists have been troublesome. The language of plants is a clearer, more coherent one than it was in the past. In the days before Linnaeus first brought order to the naming of names, the correct title for a creeping buttercup was *Ranunculus pratensis repens hirsutus* var.; a coconut was *Palma indica coccifera angulosa*. Still, given the speed with which labels and packing slips disappear around our place, I have a hard time remembering the names of my plants. If I have to remember a list of synonyms I may simply refer to *Dendranthema* 'Clara Curtis' as "the short daisy with pink flowers." I cast my lot with Mr. Philip. Autumn loses its joy without sedum.

Autumn arrives in September here, on the calendar and in the climate. Nighttime breezes scour the sky, leaving it a brilliant, polished blue; the air smells sharp and clean; rain falls with a gentle regularity; and a new round of blooms unfolds in the garden. After the hot and ragged days of August, this is the time for clear thinking and spirited activity. Fall orders begin to appear and must be planted; other plants need moving. In many ways the excitement and activity of autumn resemble the wild days of spring. But there is a difference: The lessons of summer are still fresh in the gardener's mind, giving him a sense of realism with which to tackle the future. Fall is spring with wisdom.

Although certain plants should not be disturbed in the fall, many can be planted or transplanted with ease. For some, such as peonies, fall is the best time to handle them—and the only time mail-order firms will offer them. Peonies come in a range of colors, from fiery crimsons to pale pinks and shimmering whites. I like them even now in their decline, when their leaves turn a burnished russet, the color of apples gone by. What I do not like about peonies is the tricky business of planting them. If you plant the tubers too deeply the flower buds never mature (if they appear at all), instead shriveling into black knobs. But how do you tell whether the eyes are exactly one-half inch below the surface? With a shrub, if you lay a board across the top of the planting hole you can easily determine the depth of the root ball. But a peony is smaller, and the tuber's eyes are not all at the same level. I usually plant them in the half-light of late afternoon, and as the light fades, so does my eyesight—and my confidence. Soon my nose is nearly in the dirt as I tentatively spread one-half inch of soil over the eyes of 'Sarah Bernhardt'. A firm pat and then—no, it was too firm a pat, or too much soil. The depth is not right. Up comes the tuber, and I begin again with less daylight and more uncertainty. The job is finally completed in darkness. I spread a blanket of mulch over the bed, not stopping to worry whether this upsets the half-inch equation. It doesn't; the peonies lie dormant through the winter and in spring arise and bloom with abandon.

Bulbs account for most of my planting at this time of year, and they pose no need for stewing over tape measures. If I fail to plant them deeply enough, they will haul themselves deeper into the ground. The difficulty with bulbs is making choices. One option is to choose mixtures of this or that bulb; I have followed this course, and it works fine. But this season I set out to buy an assortment of named narcissus, having been struck last spring by the distinctive character of various hybrids in friends' gardens. Beyond the obvious differences in the height of the flower stalk and the size, shape, and color of the flowers, there are many subtle differences—a slight shading of color in the leaf, a bit more frill in the trumpet, or perhaps a variation in the flower's nod. Each distinction gives character and personality to the particular plant. Scattered on the ground in September, the bulbs may seem lifeless and unremarkable, but come spring their personalities will add a special joy to the garden. It takes a gardener in autumn, with summer's lessons fresh in mind, to trust the likes of peony tubers, narcissus bulbs, and even himself.

Good fences make good neighbors, wrote Robert Frost, although as Frost well knew that is not the whole story. Fences, good or bad, also draw out other strains of personality besides neighborliness. As the tender of fences on a small city yard, I have had some chance to consider their effects. This took on the trappings of a scientific inquiry in the spring, when it was decided that we needed new fencing.

My favorite fence when I was young was broad and low, more wall than fence, and built mostly of marble and fieldstone. It started life in front of our house, as much an introduction to the driveway as a barrier to errant autos, which were more common some years ago, when the road was dirt and the winter plowing left the road a bobsled run. This elaborate structure has been moved twice since then, stone by stone, as my father has found better or more necessary sites, reassembled each time with greater finesse until now it is so tight I believe it could shed rain. It stands at the back of our land these days along the alleged boundary line. Neither my father nor his neighbor knows exactly where the line runs, but sixty feet of solid rock is a strong argument for agreement.

My city fence argues for little other than replacement. It is gray and stooped and meanders in places, not as sure on its feet as it once was. A grapevine clambers recklessly along the top of one section, ever hopeful of jumping across to the shrub rose or the mock orange that grow along the way. Down the sidewalk honeysuckle has woven itself into the chain link, forming a fence within a fence. Whether these are toppling the structure or holding it up I can't be sure, but the beauty of their lush green contours is undeniable, and the fence wears them with grace, providing a sturdy stage in return for some clothing.

At the back of the property the fence wears another sort of garland: Three strands of barbed wire festoon the top of the chain link, dividing me from my neighbor and giving new meaning to the term "spite fencing." I doubt it would deter anyone (one can always find the gate); it certainly doesn't slow the squirrels. The barbs grab hold of a tail now and then, sending a startled squirrel to the earth. The fur on their tails has grown thin from this abuse too. All the same, they lope along the wire at a crack, cheeks full of cargo found in the woodpile and destined for their treetop dwellings.

A new wooden fence will no doubt add stature to our shrub border out back. Maybe it will even turn away the English ivy that now scurries through from the neighbors'. In front, we will be able to garden in peace, hidden from all the passersby. Yet we'll no longer be able to stretch and pause to stare at these strollers or gauge the skill of a neighbor's hedge trimming. We'll lose sight of that grapevine devouring whole sections of chain link by the day. We may curb the curiosity of one or two cats, but what about the squirrels—will they take their traffic elsewhere?

I know what our reaction will be. After we've stood admiring it a few days, we'll pull out the catalogs and order a collection of clematis and a number of climbing roses, maybe a hydrangea or wisteria. And before they arrive we'll probably drive over to the local nursery and pick up one or two honeysuckle plants, just to make the fence decent in the meantime.

Starting sometime in July, about the nineteenth to be precise, I suffered a gradual but increasing indifference to my garden. The garden suffered as a result. This decline started with a vacation in early July. (Vacations are often the root of evil.) I knew it meant trouble to leave the place unattended in midsummer, and I returned ready for a struggle. It was no contest; a stretch of scorching sunny days had baked the plants and bolstered the weeds. The soil was gray and cracked, the lawn flecked with powdery mildew and crabgrass. I did a quick two-step with a scuffle hoe and applied soaker hoses, but the garden was past saving. I spent the rest of the summer mowing the lawn, weeding listlessly, and dreaming up excuses not to go home before dark. Having spent the latter half of the summer avoiding my gardens, I was thankful for the onset of autumn. The first long rains of fall—the first rains of any sort in months—and cooling temperatures brought me around; before I knew it I was heading home right after work and toiling in the gardens until well after dark.

I had told myself there would be no plants purchased and no serious alterations made in the garden this fall. But like most gardeners, on these matters I have all the conviction of a traveling salesman. I shortly found myself dragging some plants around the place on an old bed sheet and moving others a few inches this way or that to get their positions just so. Three young lilacs got snugged back against a fence, thereby improving the lot of a stand of astilbe that stood in their shadow and confirming my wife's opinion that I'd planted them wrong at the start. In the opening at the base of the lilacs went four yellow-leaved hostas, two ferns, and three epimediums. Around the corner I juggled a collection of thalictrum, some *Geranium* 'Johnson's Blue', a few slips of ivy, and two chunks of sweet woodruff. So much for holding the line on moving plants.

I have kept pretty much to the stuff about now buying new plants. My only order to date was for two *Rhododendron yakushimanum* 'Yaku Princess'. They will take the place of a group of bee balm, which I liked very much except for the powdery mildew that tore through them every year. Otherwise I'm not ordering anything. I still haven't mailed the bulb order I filled out some time back ($115 plus shipping and handling), but I'm running out of time. And the other night I toyed with the thought of calling in an order for some ajuga to fill the spaces in a stone walk.

There's plenty to be done without a boxful of adolescent plants in need of attention. For one thing, I should put away the outdoor furniture. Soon I should dump the bedraggled annuals out of their summer pots, wash the pots, and stand them to dry. While they're drying I can gather up the bamboo and plastic stakes that now support drooping carcasses. Then I can trim the withered foliage to the ground without getting poked in the eye. When that's done I'll spread a thin top dressing of compost around the garden, after which I can wash all the tools and stash them in the cellar along with the wheelbarrow, pots, stakes, lawn mower, and dibble. I should manage all these tasks this month, but I may not. There's loads to do, and with my long summer doldrums I'm running well behind schedule.

Despite appearances, a compost pile is much more than a casual mound of garden debris. Depending on your philosophy, the job of constructing one calls for the skills of a structural engineer and a chemist, the discipline of a time and motion specialist, and the intuitions of a brewmaster. Unfortunately, my initial efforts lacked most of these qualities, and the result was little more than a misshapen mound of garden remnants. So last spring I decided finally to straighten things out. It's too early to know whether the changes increased the production of compost, but they did provide me with a minor archeological adventure and a lesson in the meandering course of progress.

Back to the original pile. It started with the construction of a low wall of concrete blocks in a corner of the yard, where a trio of philadelphuses provided suitable camouflage. Into this tiny bunker I dumped most anything. In season you could find fading but still fragrant flowers of narcissi, peonies, roses, or lilacs; a dusting of lawn clippings; and oak and maple leaves.

Then last spring a friend gave me a compost machine, and I saw the chance to improve my efforts. It's a simple device, little more than a glorified fifty-gallon drum riddled with holes. According to the instructions, it bolted together in a straightforward fashion. I managed to assemble it correctly on my second try, and I stood it on its stand. (It rotates—with help—aerating the mix and spilling out finished compost all without a thought from the gardener.)

When I went to transfer the old pile into the new machine I got my first good look at the results of a couple years' decay. There was plenty of dark humus. The look and smell of the final product isn't easy to describe, but you know it when you see it and sniff it. It smells rich and healthy and has a texture that holds roots without holding them up.

Not all the pile had turned to compost. I uncovered clumps of daylily roots still alive and preparing for a new year, determined to send out a set of leaves and another crop of orange flowers, which is the reason I discarded them. Around the edges of the mound bits and pieces of forgotten (and unwanted) plants and bulbs readied themselves for another season. I sifted out labels for long-disintegrated plants. I unearthed the leathery root balls of houseplants that seemed as immune to the action of the compost pile as they had been to my attempts to keep them alive.

The new machine filled quickly, and a dusting of compost soon began to filter out of the holes and down to the ground. A friend tells me the process will go more quickly if I add in a healthy dose of twigs. I'm sure he's right, and I'm always glad to have more compost. But I'll miss tumbling around in my small mountain of garden gleanings, loosening a section here, tidying a crumbling corner there, deciding whether the ratio of large leaves to small leaves was right or whether I needed to add some privet clippings before throwing on the hosta leaves. I never thought to photograph that pile; on the other hand, I cherish the recollection of cast-off daffodils blooming in the early spring on the slope of the pile. I may still put a few daffodils in the ground, which is now lawn. They're bound to prosper in such fertile territory.

OCTOBER

THE SOUND OF FALLING LEAVES ALWAYS CATCHES ME BY surprise. It is an unmistakable noise, yet every year I am caught off guard. I become aware of a sound, irregular but constant, part rustle, part tapping. It is soft but with a certain crispness in the notes. There is a determination in this drop of leaves—gravity is a straightforward affair—and the noise is a natural piece of fall's preparation for winter.

If you watch a leaf make this free fall, it is hard to see how any noise is made. A leaf launches suddenly, quietly, drops with the delicacy of a down feather, and settles to ground as smoothly as the sun going over the horizon at day's end. Still, on a quiet day a mature maple produces a chorus of nicks and rustles.

In our garden, three trees account for most of the annual carpeting of leaves: a silver maple that reaches five, maybe six stories high, a ginkgo only slightly smaller, and a witch hazel of modest proportions. It is the decline and fall of the three that I watch for. The ginkgo turns a buttery yellow; its softly sculpted leaves seem to spill down endlessly, filling gutters and blanketing the lawn and paths at its feet. The delicate look and color of the leaves belie their sturdiness. They maintain their waxy character and remain fresh and flexible long into the autumn. They are a pleasure to look at, a pain to gather up.

The witch hazel drops its leathery leaves more quickly, and they lose their luster in a hurry. I read somewhere that witch hazels drop all their leaves at once. I have never seen this happen, but it would no doubt be a wonderful sight. The best my tree can manage is to shed itself in the course of a few days. When the tree sat in the middle of our lawn—we moved it into the garden proper—the fallen leaves formed a pool of tawny yellow in the green grass.

On the far side of the garden stands the silver maple. It is a grand and broad plant that dominates the garden throughout the year. If the leaves of the witch hazel make a pool, then those of the silver maple make a sea—with waves that move across the lawn and eddies that form in the nooks and crannies of the borders. They form wakes behind you as you plow through them. This is one of the times of year when I disregard my father's admonitions not to shuffle. (Winter is the other time, of course.) The sound and the effect of dragging your feet through a thick sea of leaves make a virtue of an otherwise bad habit.

As long as the leaves do not mat the grass too much, I simply mow them. This pulverizes them somewhat, speeding up their decay and adding nutrients to the lawn. When they become too thick, I begin raking them into piles and windrows and carting them to the compost heap. I do not greatly love raking leaves, though on a crisp autumn day the work warms you, and next to mowing, nothing gives a garden a freshly scrubbed look so quickly. But once done, the job must soon be repeated. The work is endless and dull, but the reward is a layer of rich leaf mold come spring. It is a pleasant if pedestrian reminder of the sights and sounds of fall, and one more reason for growing trees.

I recently cut down a birch tree. It was a modest tree, perhaps twenty-five feet high and as many years old. It had been dead for some time, so the decision to cut it down was a sensible one; all the same, I hesitated and felt a wave of guilt as the chain saw bit into the trunk. Cutting down trees has that effect on gardeners. The very idea paralyzes even the most hardened people, folks for whom making tough decisions is a matter of daily course. Some people adopt a policy of not cutting down any tree—no matter what. Once a tree takes hold, they simply work around it. They will spare even Norway maples, greedy, weedy trees that as a group should be culled from the landscape.

Maybe it is the sense of permanence that trees convey that makes people reluctant to cut them down. I imagine even loggers with a lifetime of felling trees behind them get wishy-washy at the prospect of taking one out of the backyard. The trouble—or should we say trauma—has nothing to do with the fear of getting hurt or splitting the house in two with a poorly aimed tree. It has to do with notions of our natural legacy and respect for age.

Nature must have foreseen our waffling ways, for she saw to it that the job of removing trees from the landscape was not left entirely to us. Weak and sickly trees that we do not or will not deal with are usually brought down by storms, which cull the landscape with swift and dispassionate objectivity. Every couple years a hurricane sweeps along the East Coast and brings down thousands of trees. They are missed, no doubt, but probably not for long. In Great Britain, unexpected hurricanes mauled the land in 1987 and 1989, tearing hundreds of thousands of trees from the ground, many of them centuries old and in that sense irreplaceable. Before too long, however, British gardeners began to admit that the storms performed a valuable job that no one had the courage to consider, much less carry out. Vistas reappeared for the first time in decades. Clogged gardens suddenly enjoyed a sense of light and openness. And borders that were full to bursting gained open space for new specimens. One writer commented that the storm mocked the idea of trees as low-maintenance plants.

Gardens grow more slowly than we generally prefer but more quickly than we often realize. While we bury our heads in our borders, the trees and shrubs slowly make their way upward and outward. A view to the corner of the garden or to a field beyond is lost and soon forgotten, and the garden is diminished.

The decision to cut down the birch was a simple one; borers had already killed it, and I was simply in charge of cleaning it up. But my garden is another story. It is overplanted in the fashion of any acquisitive gardener. A dogwood is beginning to elbow a witch hazel, which is in turn threatened by a weeping katsura. Some plants will be moved, others discarded altogether. It seems a heartless attitude, perhaps, but it is little more than what goes on in the perennial border. Removing things from the garden is as important, though not as fun, as putting things in.

It isn't normal to look forward to winter, and I cannot say I'm on the edge of my seat awaiting its arrival. But I am curious to see what our new pergola looks like come February. At the moment it looks new, and I am always aware of it standing there behind the vegetable garden like some awkward visitor. The hope is that under the influence of time and weather it will come to be noticeable but not out of place, a feature but not an eyesore.

If the actual structure looks awkward in its youth, the idea made sense from the start. A pergola coming off a door out of the garage and running along the length of the vegetable garden would add height, intricacy, and architecture to the garden. We could cover it with grapes or roses or whatever appealed to us. So last fall I excavated two rows of five holes on eight-foot centers. The digging went easily enough. When the work was finished, with bamboo stakes marking the placement of the posts-to-be and crisp white string tracing the parallel outline of the posts, the job seemed nearly complete. Then came winter, and the string sagged and turned gray; the bamboo posts tilted in odd directions. By spring the sides of the holes, once neatly vertical, crumbled and gave way. By May weeds covered the mounds of soil I'd dug up. It looked more like the site of unsuccessful oil and gas drillings than the start of an architectural gem.

Luckily at the start of spring I had come across a man in southern Vermont who had a crop of black locust poles the right length (ten feet) and diameter (five to six inches). I arranged to purchase forty poles. My first look at them was discouraging. They looked as thick as telephone poles but nowhere near as straight. And each one weighed well over 100 pounds. My plan of erecting a pergola easily and alone quickly disappeared.

I called Bill Desimone, who runs a contracting company with his brother Dave. Usually they build houses and such, but they seem to draw some amusement out of the oddball projects my wife and I occasionally propose to them. The two made quick work of the job. The first day they set the uprights, using a transit to get all the holes square and true; that evening the area looked full of possibilities, an idea taking shape but not yet flawed with finality. Then they notched and fitted the lintels and rafters. Finally the whole arrangement was secured with shiny, twelve-inch lag bolts.

With any new undertaking, acceptance comes gradually. The pergola isn't exactly what I imagined last winter, but I enjoy the look of it more every day. The poles are as straight as any tree Nature creates, and the slight swellings and undulations of the individual poles are no more than character lines. The vegetable garden no longer floats in the lawn, and the garage looks suddenly much more important. I took some photographs and showed them to Barker Willard, the young man who helped me load the logs in Vermont. Barker is a builder who knows about pergolas. He scanned them and nodded his quiet approval. Emily and I haven't yet decided what to grow on the pergola, but even so I agree with Barker that "it didn't come out half bad."

The great consolation in any gardening enterprise is that the plants will make every effort to survive and prosper, no matter what obstacles the weather or the gardener can throw in their way. That is not to say the gardener does not have it within his powers to thwart a growing plant. Indeed, much of a gardener's education involves learning to stay out of the way. Having been at the task for centuries, most plants need only occasional and elementary bits of assistance to grow.

The difficulty comes in making a garden out of all the assorted plants a gardener gathers around himself. This garden must bloom for most of the year (starting immediately), withstand flying soccer balls and wandering dogs, take care of itself, and do all this in a site that is too small, too dark, and either too cold or too warm. Say you're attracted to hostas and hemerocallis and Japanese maples; can you work them all into a garden together? Maybe you want all small plants or all tall ones, maybe nothing but red flowers or a combination of reds and blues. Is there a way to work some flowers into your vegetable garden, or an arrangement that allows you more plants where you have less space?

Now, you can forget trying to answer all those questions and simply plant things wherever you find bare earth and then move them to different spots later on. This method slows erosion and allows the gardener plenty of time for tennis, but it does not make a pleasing garden, at least not very quickly. Following this course, I placed a group of *Lobelia ×vedrariensis* behind a cluster of *Hemerocallis* 'Madame Chang' last spring. The lobelia flowers are described as a brilliant purple, and if brilliant also means lurid that is a fair description. I'm sure this hybrid deserves a place in the garden, but its vibrant shade grated against the more delicate hues of 'Madame Chang'. In the fall I put it elsewhere. Likewise I had to move a specimen of *Hosta fortunei* 'Robusta' that I had planted the previous spring next to a young *Acer palmatum* var. *dissectum* 'Garnet'. The broad, spreading leaves of the hosta threatened to dwarf the delicate weeping maple, and there was nothing appealing in the association. The whole arrangement looked out of balance, a failure in creative contrast.

Elsewhere in my garden another large-leaved blue hosta contributed to a different, this time successful, composition. The hosta stood at a corner of the garden, with stone paths on two sides. On the other two sides were a group of *Heuchera* 'Pluie de Feu' and one of *Geranium ×oxonianum* 'Wargrave Pink'. As spring progressed the geranium spread beneath the hosta, carpeting the open ground beneath it. In late June when the coralbells flowered their cherry-red bloom stalks poked up among the large hosta leaves. The small, delicate heuchera flowers, which often disappear against a less uniform background, were at once highlighted and softened by the blue-gray hosta leaves. It may seen odd or garish to some, but I admired the simple elegance and only wished I'd dreamed it up.

Whatever form it takes, the placement of plants in the garden is all-important. It is the essence of garden design. It is the source of character and (one hopes) pleasure in a garden.

On the radio recently, writer Daniel Pinkwater, a fellow who talks openly about his substantial weight, referred to himself not as fat but as "circumferentially challenged" and "diametrically disadvantaged." This politically correct thinking got me wondering about how my garden stands up to the tests of political correctness. Judging from the weeds, I would say it is a wildflower-friendly spot. Looking at the tiny yews around the kitchen garden, you would certainly say they're altitudinally challenged. We have a lawn that is verdancy impaired. That collection of pots on the stone steps—is it a riot of color or just chromatically courageous?

Certain terms are clearly appropriate for an upstanding gardener intent on exhibiting a knowledge of good gardening. Nobody likes invasive plants; far better to term them vigorous weavers and minglers. That pile of debris towering alongside the garage, why, that's the compost pile. Earthworms, too, have gained new currency. Discussions of compost piles often involve debates on the merits of annelids such as *Lumbricus terrestris* (the common earthworm) or *Eisenia foetida* (the manure or brandling worm). It's also a sign of a good gardener to show an affection for bats and squirrels. Not long ago I visited a friend whose neighbor has posted ten bat houses around his property, and down in Washington, D.C., squirrel seats and toys are showing up in notable gardens.

Going native is also appropriate for gardeners. Turning your lawn into a wildflower meadow is a sign of high sensibility. Weeds are now glorified for their ancestry: Joe-pye weed, for example, is considered a perfect plant for the back of the border, and gardeners eagerly tout their favorite goldenrods, although nowadays they insist on calling them solidagos. While Latin remains a key to proper horticultural conversation, the matter of pronunciation is thorny and controversial. Some folk hold that the proper way to pronounce forsythia is for-SIGH-thee-ah; after all, that's how William Forsyth said his name. And others would insist you pronounce bergenia, burr-GEN-ee-a, not burr-JEEN-ee-a, presumably because that is how Carl von Bergen would have wanted it. Such perfection requires an ability to roll r's in a rumbling Germanic fashion that eludes me.

On the matter of things foreign there is no clear course of

correct behavior. British books generally are to be shunned, as is any display of Anglophilia. But French beans, Japanese radishes, and most other vegetables of foreign origin are acceptable. South Africa, although it has a precarious government, is a Mecca for plant lovers. Plants from there, and from New Zealand and neighboring Australia, are all worth knowing. Many are drought tolerant, a desirable trait, and produce vibrant flowers. Hot colors are no longer scorned—call them visually stirring.

The problem with all of this is that so many matters are not clearly right or wrong. Take lawn mowers. There are Good Mowers (all mulching models) and Bad Mowers (those that cough blue smoke and are louder than passing trucks). With a birthday in the offing, I am conscious of becoming ever more chronologically enhanced, and I think occasionally of trading in the push mower for something with a seat and a steering wheel. On the other hand, maybe I'll just get myself a bench of nonendangered wood, settle back, and watch the whole patch go natural.

Unless you fancy the heavy hue of a Paris streetwalker's lipstick, the brilliant red of annual salvias may strike you as overwhelming. They may not affect others that way, but their riotous reds make me blink and grimace. Nevertheless, I accepted a gift of some robust young seedlings from a friend last spring. Just why I agreed to take them is a mystery to me, for as soon as I got them home I knew that the sensible decision would be to cart them right away to the compost heap. Scarlet red is not a color that mixes easily. If it goes anywhere, it goes by itself, though I would prefer that it just go elsewhere.

I am by no means opposed to any and all reds, even brilliant ones. I think a cluster of 'Red Emperor' tulips (or a mass of them if you can afford it) brightens the landscape without insult, although I do know people who would rather stare directly at an eclipse. For some reason, however, the sight of the fiery reds of salvias like 'Red Blazer' or 'Hot Shot' or 'Blaze of Fire' fills me with horror, and I pity the poor copywriters who inherit the task of stringing together a few good words about these annuals. These folks are clever and make the best of a grim situation, calling the blossoms "brilliant," "superb," and "intense"; but one should not fall for this, nor for their praise of the striking, glossy foliage, the long season, and the sturdy character of the plants. All these claims are true, but the traits are not necessarily ones a gardener wants in a plant. (In fairness, I should mention that I enjoy some of the other colors of *Salvia splendens*: the lavenders, salmons, pinks, blues, even some of the violets. All of them conduct themselves with admirable grace and unexpected moderation.)

By the middle of September my grove of 'Blaze of Fire' was blooming so relentlessly that I became convinced even the killing frosts would not halt its display. To make matters worse, the salvia was but one element of a design that I had concluded was a hellish tapestry of stubby blues, lurid reds, and strident yellows. So one afternoon I took my garden fork out to turn over the whole patch and give the neighborhood some visual relief.

While I was standing at the garden's edge trying to recall what had possessed my sense of aesthetics last spring, something flew into the salvia. For a moment I couldn't make out what it was. It flew with too much speed and dexterity to be a moth; it was too late for a bee yet too small for a bird. In another second I realized it was a hummingbird, a female, come to drink from my 'Blaze of Fire'. With its tail weaving and bobbing and its wings in a near-motionless blur, the bird sampled five or six plants, zipping away between sips in great boomeranging arcs across the street. She seemed not to notice my presence, so I stood there, five feet away, and relished her dizzying performance while she moved about the salvia.

She left as abruptly as she arrived; the whole event lasted a little longer than a minute. It was my first meeting with a hummingbird, and it was enough to change my heart about the salvia. How could a passing hummingbird miss the neon welcome of 'Blaze of Fire'? Next spring, if I can find the space, I think I'll tuck a few 'Hot Shot's into my garden on the chance that a hummingbird comes looking for a feast.

November

NOVEMBER IS A LINGERING MONTH, BOTH FOR THE garden and for the gardener. To the north and west the season has shifted to winter plain and simple, but here by the coast winter comes later and more gradually. The mornings are cold and frosty, afternoons close in early. But there are still many plants standing in the garden, and when the sun is out you think more of fall than of winter. I often wake up shivering and decide that today I will clean the garden for the year. Then the sun comes around the hill and up over the neighbors' roofs and persuades me to hold off until a colder day. Besides, other jobs need doing before winter arrives at least and (so it seems) for good.

The grasses are still standing, their flowers waving like tattered pennants raised proudly against the approach of winter. Worst off is *Miscanthus sinensis* 'Zebrinus'. Flowering seems to take all the starch out of this plant, for it splays and flops early in fall, looking beaten rather than tousled. Not so for *Calamagrostis acutiflora* 'Stricta', the flower stalks of which remain ramrod straight above a mound of scruffy foliage. Silvery spines of *Helictotrichon sempervirens* and burgundy *Imperata cylindrica* var. *rubra* are still interesting, the one ghostly against the browns and grays of surrounding plants, the other giving off a pale-rose glow in the angled light. Taken together, the grasses stand about the garden like a company of scarecrows, cheerful and resolute.

No matter the date or whether killing frost has yet occurred (it usually has), various plants bravely put out flowers. The most dependable plant in my garden for this activity is the rose 'Betty Prior', which blooms into December, with pinkish-red flowers scattered about lanky stems and set against dark leaves, now tarnished and tattered. At its feet is a great ghostly mound of *Artemisia* 'Powis Castle'. This plant has tender blood in its veins and doesn't survive the winter. But it lives well into the fall without flagging. When I finally cut it down, it fills the chill air with a delicate perfume, an exotic scent at this time of year.

Any number of tender geraniums (pelargoniums) continue to bloom. Bushy and studded with bloom in July, these plants are now gangly. Their crooked stems flop over the sides of the pots I grow them in, spilling to the ground but throwing out blossoms of velvet red. A cold night may turn the flowers to mush, but a warm day will bring out a few more. When I finally tip them out onto the compost pile, they struggle on, chiding me for giving up so easily.

But there are jobs to be done, and some of these—such as getting the pots indoors before a truly fierce frost shatters them—cannot wait much longer. Late-arriving lilies must be planted, and the soil, no longer so warm, makes clear that this year's planting days are numbered. One by one, plants will drop their last leaves. The Siberian irises will topple in a heap; the burnished mounds of hardy geraniums will fall flat. So too the astrantias, leaving a limp mass that must be pried off the ground. When these plants finally collapse, I will wonder why I held off putting things in order. But then, while stuffing a few stray tulips into the garden, I will come across a flower of some aster or rudbeckia, or maybe an annual buried beneath fallen maple leaves. That flower is usually ragged, but there it is, a colorful argument that autumn may well be the longest season.

It's not often that gardeners find themselves ahead of schedule, especially when it comes to making their fall rounds. But every once in a while we get a jump on the season, thanks to the rare visit of a hurricane. One notable example was the year Gloria came to town. She deserves thanks for coming. She shook me free from the listless state I had settled into halfway through August. She also shook free a number of unwanted branches high in our maple tree, saving me a dangerous job. By neatly leveling a great number of plants in the course of an hour's stay, she brought an abrupt halt to the summer, giving both the garden and the gardener a needed kick in the seat.

I had half hoped Gloria might prove a tonic for the garden, which looked weary and ragged after a summer thin on rain and thick on aphids and other infestations. She arrived somewhat exhausted by the journey north. All the same, she thrashed around for a couple hours, broke branches, toppled a piece of topiary, and closed out the season for two young peonies. Even for an aging hurricane she made a strong impression. I will not soon forget the sight of our old trees rocking back and forth like young saplings.

Gloria moved on quickly, leaving behind a lawn badly in need of grooming. If you own a small yard you know that such jobs must be taken up promptly. Leave them for later, and they will mock your good intentions every time you step out the front door. At first I tried hiding all the debris behind a clump of hemlocks in one corner of our yard, but there was more litter than space.

Pretty soon I went down to the cellar and hauled out our shredder, a German machine I bought one day last spring. I had been overcome by visions of homemade compost and promises that this machine could reduce my yard to a pile the size of a four-inch pot. In its small way, the machine works with a fury not unlike Gloria's, although the noise it makes is coarse and complaining by comparison. You need little skill to operate this shredder (the manufacturer's guarantee is longer than the operating instructions); all you need are gloves and protection for your eyes and ears. It has the eating habits of a snake, swallowing large bites and then taking hours to pass them through its system. This is fine for the constrictors but not for gardeners with other jobs to finish. As for the results, I have heard that Thalassa Cruso suggests storing them in a closet. Unfortunately we're short on closets. I might sneak a pile behind the woodpile for the winter, or at the end of the driveway—if I can spread the mound of mulch already sitting there.

As you can tell, the laws of energy have been hard at work here, what with the winds coming in and tossing around branches, the gardener using up energy (his own and the power company's) raking and shredding and moving piles back and forth. It's a lucky break Gloria got here early; otherwise fall chores could have gone on until well past Christmas.

Groundcovers, like so many other things, are good for you in moderation. Sadly, gardeners often think of them as a tactic of last resort, a solution for desperate circumstances, and employ them all or nothing. The result is great sweeps of pachysandra as interesting as a desert. Such planting does a disservice to the garden as well as the pachysandra.

Our house was surrounded by groundcovers when we arrived. Vinca blanketed the ground along the front fence. The front had sides of the house were surrounded by luxuriant beds of pachysandra. Ivy ('Baltic', I believe, but have no way of knowing for sure) claimed the ground along the back of the property (and most of a six-foot-high fence and a forty-foot-high Norway maple for good measure). We spent a large portion of our first season peeling back these covers. I suspect we shredded and composted ten wheelbarrow loads of ivy and pachysandra. The vinca we largely gave away to a friend across town. After rebuilding the soil we began planting, covering up the bare soil as Nature intended soil to be treated.

Although the plantings are more varied and more formal than the groundcovers they replaced, many of the plants display some of the more desirable traits of those groundcovers. They are strong growers, long-lived, and they do cover ground. Some—like alchemillas, campanulas, and corydalis—seed themselves around freely, filling in the open soil with greater or lesser speed. Many others creep and crawl from their original location—polygonatums, epimediums, hemerocallis, ferns, violas, ajugas, and hardy geraniums, to name only a few. Yet others such as bergenias, hostas, hellebores, and astilbes stay put for the most part but will form a dense cover. The list of plants that fall under these headings is long, even for northern gardens. They are all desirable plants; many of them belong in any garden, no matter what their role. That they keep weeds down and live long lives only adds to their value. Few of the plants are so invasive (or few of the gardens so grand) that their spread cannot be easily curbed. Some of the violas, maybe, ivy perhaps. But you can pluck vagrant corydalis without trouble. And no geranium can outrun a gardener, even in midsummer.

The trick with these plants is to give them an inch without letting them take a mile. Let them wander, covering bald spots and difficult areas, knitting together the garden but not over-whelming it. What you get is surely not a low-maintenance garden; on the other hand, if you plan ahead you can achieve such seamless designs as, for example, *Epimedium rubrum* spread under and around the arching wands of variegated Solomon's seal, or a *Geranium endresii* wound into and up onto the yellow-edged foliage of *Hosta* 'Frances Williams'. The combinations are countless, the results often unexpectedly appealing.

The plants need not be uncommon to be interesting. The glossy, sharply cut leaves of *Pachysandra terminalis* or the creep-ing tendrils of euonymus or the jagged blue-green branches of juniper can contribute to an exciting garden if you allow them to mingle with others instead of relegating them to a plot of their own. All that's needed is a gardener with a creative spirit and a firm grip on a trowel.

You cannot make a good garden without trees. They add height and heft, shade and privacy. You can grow all sorts of plants up into their branches, and many minor bulbs are best seen clustered at their feet. They offer color—in their flowers, their foliage, and their bark. I would include trees in my gar-den if only to hear the wind sifting through their leaves. In the morning I listen to hear what the trees have to tell me about the weather; is it the soft rustle of a friendly day, or rough-and-tumble lashing of a storm? Trees expand the horizons of a gar-den in almost innumerable ways, and there are almost as many trees as there are reasons for growing them.

I was relieved, all the same, to find only five trees in our new garden. We had inherited more than a dozen with our old garden, leaving little chance for any additions. In the new garden we have a towering Norway maple and a chokecherry, which will stay; a smaller Norway maple and a weedy crab apple, both of which will come down this winter; and a majestic ginkgo, which could make a garden by itself. It is a male and therefore lacks the fruit, which, in the words of one writer, is "definitely not ornamental."

Choosing trees for a garden is more difficult and yet more enjoyable than selecting shrubs or perennials, if that is possible. The stakes are greater (as is the cost), the margin for error is considerably less, and the options increase dramatically with each year. These factors together with my own spotty knowledge have kept me busy through the fall. I am hunting for a few conifers to cluster along the back of one long border. These evergreens are often relegated to the position of lone sentinels or anonymous windbreaks. Gardeners don't often allow them into the nicer neighborhoods of their gardens, which is a disservice to both the conifers and the gardens. They provide strong shapes and gentle colors that other plants rarely match, especially in winter. Some are nicely fragrant. There is hardly a bad plant among their ranks (*Chamaecyparis* and *Taxus* included); they deserve wider use in gardens.

The prospects among the deciduous trees are also vast, filled with little-known gems. You can choose among the many magnolias (one friend is insisting on a 'Merrill'), the undervalued hawthorns, and the quince. I would love a grove of willows and an avenue of crab apples ('Donald Wyman' and 'Golden Hornet' rank high on my list). There will also be a place for a maple—not a Norway but a paperbark (*Acer griseum*), a mild-mannered tree that grows to twenty-five feet and has elegant exfoliating bark.

My favorite tree of the moment is a little-known locust. *Robinia pseudoacacia* 'Frisia' is a modest-size tree that gives the open shade common to this native American family. Its greatest asset is the foliage, a golden yellow that holds throughout the summer. It is a more vibrant color than that of *Gleditsia triacanthos* 'Sunburst'. The tree is in size and spirit well suited to a smaller garden. A few nurseries offer it irregularly; I think I have got my hands on a plant.

I doubt I'll see it or most of these trees until spring. That's actually all for the good; it should take me the better part of the winter to figure out who goes where.

The ground in early fall still holds the heat of July and August, and the sensation of digging your hands into the soil on a chill morning is like reaching into a faintly warm oven. With the sun just breaking over the horizon and your breath visible in the air, the temperature a few inches belowground is in the sixties, fine for plants as well as fingers. By the start of November, though, the summer's warmth is mostly gone out of the soil. There is little pleasure in working in it and small chance of survival for most new plantings. I warm myself instead with the chores of readying the garden for winter.

Bedding down my garden is not the great task it is for those gardeners who insist on wraps and coverings, windbreaks and snow shields. Most of my plants must survive with little more than a light mulch and a late watering. I coddle a few individuals—mainly last-minute arrivals to the garden. A collection of primroses was the final thing I planted this year; I mulched them with salt-marsh hay, knowing that nonetheless some surely will heave out of the ground before winter finishes. I also trussed up two Ellwood's chamaecyparis with jute twine to protect their supple branches from the snow that pries them open.

Mostly the work goes on away from the garden. All the ornaments and implements that fill and fortify the borders through the summer need to be gathered and stored. The supports I so carefully hid in spring must now be untangled from the remains of peonies, erodiums, thalictrums, and irises. The pots filled with lilies, lobelias, nasturtiums, helichrysums, and the like need to be retrieved—the tattered plantings added to the compost pile—then washed and stacked in an appropriate spot. This is the routine I envision. But a pot or two always escapes my notice, and I only discover them after their contents have frozen and become locked inside. Last December I discovered a pot of clivia sitting, like a fledgling animal, on a little-used porch. I brought it inside and thawed it in a bowl next to a radiator until I could tip out the icy chunk of soil and leaves.

Even at this time of year I am still dealing with the lawn-mower, which has been my weekly companion since sometime in late April. After one last mowing, done mostly to mulch leaves and use up any gas remaining in the tank, I leave the mower running and go about other work while it purrs its way to empty.

Toward the end of the month I will make one last effort to lodge various plant labels deep into the ground with hope of defeating the endless push of frost that scatters them about the borders. About the same time I will water those young shrubs and trees that need help to survive the dehydrating effects of the sunny days of winter. Done in bits and pieces, the process takes a couple days, and at this time of year I leave the hose stretched across the lawn; by morning it is sometimes rigid with frost and I must work my way along its length, massaging the life back into it before I can start watering again.

The last items to go into the garage are the trowels and the garden spade and fork. They accompany me to the end of the season, repairing ragged border edges, breaking new bits of ground, planting a few last tulips found at the back of the refrigerator. I scrub the tools clean, rub the handles with linseed oil, and head indoors to dwell among the catalogs and books.

While people in the woods to the north cut and store firewood, I worry about clearing of another sort. I am in the business of felling miscanthus and iris, joe-pye weed and thalictrum. By this time the wind and rain and cold have taken the starch out of most of the plants, and the garden has gone from a ruddy, tousled look to one of tattered collapse. The changeover happens gradually, with some parts of the garden disintegrating sooner than others. But by the time the stalks of the zebra grass begin to split apart like the staves of a barrel coming unglued, the hostas will be sagging to the ground and the sedums will be splayed out onto the lawn like weary derelicts. Then there is no choice but to cut down everything and wheel it to the compost bins. It is a tedious job, one that I don't relish, but it benefits the compost, and, like the work of chopping firewood, will improve my lot in seasons to come. It also leaves the garden with its skeleton revealed, which is a refreshing sight.

The late-autumn garden is a different character from the autumn garden, a subject of much-deserved acclaim. The autumn garden is still energetic, if a little worn after a long summer of hard work. New flowers are blooming. There are asters and rudbeckias, buddleias, *Artemisia lactiflora*, and more. The foliage, though tarnished by cool temperatures and shortening days, glistens with the heavy dews. The shapes and textures of the garden are still visible and strong. In the late-autumn garden, on the other hand, all but a few stray flowers are spent, as are most of the leaves. A clump of tall white flower stalks marks the summer glory of *Hosta* 'Krossa Regal'. The hardy geraniums are a rats' nest of five months' worth of stems. The stems of balloon flower, brilliant yellow just a couple of weeks back, are drained of color and topple over one another in a tangled mass. It is a desolate scene of blackened leaves and broken stems.

Alternately singed by frost and soaked by rain, many of the plants have the consistency of well-done spaghetti. All you need to do is grab a handful of stems, give a quick tug, and a mushy gob of plant comes free. The daylilies and sedums, sturdy throughout the summer, can be raked up in great sticky clumps. Others, such as *Coreopsis verticillata* and the epimediums, though delicate in appearance, stand firm. Their blackened stems bristle as you brush them.

As the work of cutting down the borders progresses, piles grow on the lawn along the edges. There are orderly stacks of iris and blue oat grass foliage, and the still-sturdy stems of joe-pye weed, heleniums, and phlox. There are lumpy mounds of lady's mantle, geraniums, artemisias, and assorted annuals. Herbs scent the cool air with faint aromas. Late flowers peek from the piles. The compost bins will bulge with this harvest of leftovers, an early Thanksgiving feast for a myriad of worms, slugs, bugs, and beetles.

By month's end there is little left of the summer's thick layers and the bones of the garden show boldly. The hedges cast stark shadows across the close-cropped lawn. The shrubs' silhouettes are outlined against the sky. A dark line traces the curves of the borders' edges as they wind around the garden. Almost unnoticed in this spare scene are the outlines of next year's pleasures: the tidy rosettes of yarrow, campanula, and others; the tight buds of viburnums and witch hazels.

DECEMBER

YOU WOULDN'T THINK OF OUR PROPERTY AS A WOOD-
lot. It's not very big and not very wooded and claims only four
trees of substance: a towering silver maple, a great burly
ginkgo, a disheveled chokecherry, and a Norway maple, about
which there is nothing good to say except that it adds a fiery
glow to the autumn landscape. We manage, though, to glean a
good deal of wood from the place as a result of acts of God; the
wayward behavior of the sanitation trucks, which regularly tear
branches from the trees along the street; and our own efforts.
There isn't enough accumulation to keep us in decent fires
through the winter. The pieces are generally small and the
wood is poor for burning. All the same, it's amazing how much
wood you can gather from a small place and how many uses you

can put it to. It's a low-grade form of recycling, and a reassuring reminder that the land is plentiful, even in an urban environment and even when you're not looking.

Last winter, thanks to some early and wet snowfalls, we ended up with a considerable cache of wood. A storm in December leveled a stand of lilacs. The wood didn't offer much in the way of burning, but we used some of the branches to prop up geraniums, penstemons, echinops, campanulas, and the like. Other bits of brush were employed in the vegetable garden to mark planting sites and to support beans and peas. The same storm also toppled an old crab apple. One main trunk was bent to the ground and had to be cut off, and a few large pieces from this surgery went to the woodpile. I fed the debris to the chipper and then spread the results around a cluster of hollies, which stand next to the amputated crab apple.

In the same corner of the garden stand the silver maple and the chokecherry. The maple spreads its branches a great distance and its roots even more so. The chokecherry showers hard black fruits down on the garden and lawn, giving you the feeling of walking across a field of granola. Both trees scatter limbs throughout the winter—and the summer, for that matter—in a constant process of self-cleaning. For all my grousing about this, we do collect a fair amount for chipping and staking, and the deadfall never seems to damage the garden. I suppose I ought to view their contributions more generously. Still, I dream occasionally about taking a more aggressive role in recycling these two profligate thugs.

This winter I plan to take out one of the chokecherry's three trunks. Even at that, the tree may still have two too many. And there is no doubt that the time has come to cut down the crab apple. It sputtered to life in the spring and even flowered sparsely. It was a last gasp, however, the final flurry of an already dead tree. Through the hot and dry summer its leaves withered one by one. By August all that remained were a few pale leaves and some lonesome suckers. In its best days the bent and gnarled trunks lent a quality of age and character to the garden; by summer's end they had become an eyesore, a stark symbol of a winter with lots of snow and a summer with little rain. Once the ground and our resolve harden, we will drop the tree and store the cut wood in the garage. We can then look forward to a winter evening a year or two from now when we can light a fire and perhaps catch a fleeting scent of this old friend, which, when the garden was no more than a vast scattering of green nubbins, gave it character and a sense of place.

That Christmas falls in December is a wonderful coincidence for gardeners. Gardeners, I think, enjoy holidays, though not necessarily the common ones such as Patriot's Day or New Year's Day or Halloween. They reserve their celebrations for the Day the First Crocus Appeared and the Arrival of Seeds Day. The First Lilac Flower is occasion for putting aside all work. For that matter, the first of anything generally brings on some rejoicing: the first ear of corn, the first tomato, the first rhododendron or rose blossom. They will also declare a holiday, in a more melancholy spirit, to honor the last peas or the final flower on the clematis.

Gardeners are not averse to traditional holidays. Memorial Day means planting time to northerners, and on the Fourth of July they check to see if their corn is knee-high. Many consider Columbus Day the ideal time to plant bulbs.

The blessing of Christmas has nothing to do with activities in the garden, at least not around here. The ground is locked up solid, the lawn scruffy and bumpy. The trees are bare except for a few fruits clinging bravely to the crab apple and the viburnum. What's cheering about Christmas is that it provides a great bounty of gardening catalogs. Almost daily they arrive in twos or threes, quickly rising to a hefty pile. These are not the seed catalogs for spring orders; those will appear in a few weeks. This round of catalogs is a new hybrid offering plants and other sundries for gardeners at Christmas.

Finding a good present for a fellow gardener can be a tough act, and the catalogs are welcome on those grounds alone. But a sensible gardener will realize it's a good time to add to his own collection. This year, for example, at the end of an order of amaryllis for some friends I tagged on a few items for our mantelpiece: a collection of six amaryllises, a bagful of narcissi, one ornamental pot that caught my attention, and a new trowel I'd been eyeing for some months.

The offering of these holiday catalogs ranges far and wide, in some cases straying far beyond the bounds of normal horticultural territory. There are cheeses and hams, pound cakes and tree ornaments. But for the most part the selections are the sort of things a gardener needs or at least wants to carry him through until spring, all suggesting that the proprietors of these catalogs know the deprivation of winter. The pages are flush with bulbs for forcing, colorful tropical hibiscuses that bloom no matter what, topiary for fussing over, and books for browsing through. You can spend thousands on a collection of Japanese maples or a more modest sum on a Sussex trug. Sign up for a limited edition of prints or a packet of baby-vegetable seeds. There is teak and delftware in abundance, crisply cut crystal, and mirror-smooth stones from Japan. You might choose a redwood bower (eight and a half feet high, with two benches built in) or a marble turtle (eleven inches high and sluggish). Although you may buy nothing more than the same hyacinth you ordered last year, it's fun to dream about the other things. At a time when the yard is blank and gray, your imagination is free to wander at will, building ponds and setting out groves of magnolias (though spring will prove there's barely room for another tulip). This excuse for dreaming is a welcome holiday for any gardener.

One of the pleasant results of the stern New England climate at this season is a surplus of time for reading. In the summer, few days pass when I don't pull down a gardening book from its perch, hoping to convince myself that a recently hatched scheme has certain merit, or none at all. In truth, though, this activity cannot pass for reading; I invariably begin at the end, in the index, read through the page or paragraph I am looking for, and am done. You might call it the "deli" style of reading, a technique familiar to gardeners with a mission.

A gardener's library increases slowly yet undeniably, for one can usually summon a strong argument to buy every new title. Either a book promises answers to long-standing questions— the sensible use of orange flowers in a garden, say—or else some new interest takes hold in the gardener, and he is at once off hunting for a book on the topic. Actually a number of books is preferable, since they will certainly disagree with one another, thereby adding to the gardener's plentiful supply of indecision and fueling his investigations through the coming winter.

The collection of gardening books at our house fills a number of shelves plus a scattering of desk tops and side tables. Among my favorites are a large group of books that were written by authorities in the field; I rarely consult them on practical matters, preferring instead to wander through the color photographs. The reason, as you may have guessed, is that these books are imports, most of them written originally for an English audience, and unless you live on Martha's Vineyard or maybe in Seattle or Portland, they can do little but dampen your spirits on a dull day in December. The gardener in Oshkosh, full of hope and questions, who picks up such a book will be discouraged to learn he ought to plant camellias or perhaps fuchsias for that hedge he is planning. And if he is not put off, and thinks the idea worth trying, he probably won't find the particular cultivars in any of his catalogs. It is a dangerous tactic, putting a book like this in the hands of a gardener already nearing his limits with four months still to go before spring.

Neither the author nor the importer means to lead the reader on a wild goose chase; most publishers hire American editors specifically to avoid this trouble. However, the cost and the time involved in making a full translation of an import are so great that the books are still full of plants and planting ideas that won't work in some parts of this country. The reader is left largely on his own, sifting sound and broadly applicable principles from an array of examples that, if duplicated, would bring most gardens to ruin. Luckily, this intrepid behavior is commonplace among gardeners, and most come away from these imports with a great many useful ideas and nothing worse than a slight case of envy.

Although we buy imported gardening books by the truckload as if no others existed, American gardeners have contributed many fine volumes to the field. Some of them, sadly, came and retired quickly; still other excellent books have filled their places. The writing of gardeners such as Henry Mitchell, Thalassa Cruso, Allen Lacy, George Schenk, Wayne Winterrowd, and Tovah Martin, to name a few I admire, has added immensely to our skill and enjoyment. Their books add a bright and cheerful voice to the winter landscape and deserve a spot on every gardener's bookshelf.

For all its festivity and levity, Christmas is a time fraught with trying decisions, and none is more difficult than the choice of a Christmas tree. This decision grows harder by the year, as the trees of Christmas past grow taller and fuller and more richly scented in memory.

Our family's annual outing was no trifling junket. As far as my father was concerned, the pursuit of a Christmas tree was a pilgrimage of almost greater significance than the holiday itself. It involved the better part of a Saturday and included not only our family but three or four others—sometimes more, depending on who was in town. Certainly we could count on having the Finlays, the Meachams, and the Skinners along. If no one else joined our troop, that meant eight adults and nine children—which gave us children an unspoken sense of equality and responsibility in the venture. Our itinerary normally took us to a farm in the next town, where the hillsides were thick with stands of various conifers. If the snow was not overly deep we would drive the car (cars at that time didn't take well to snow) into a back field and spread out from there onto the hills.

After a spell of tromping around and getting an idea of the prospects, family members began calling one another to consider likely prospects, their voices ringing out in the forest. As the trees were clotted together in tight clusters, and because the choice of a tree is extremely personal anyway, every tree was judged from all sides by each member of a family. The possibilities of pruning and positioning a tree to fit a particular room's dimensions were hashed over, one tree's strengths and weaknesses weighed against those of other trees already in contention. When a decision was finally reached, with resolve but always some remorse, we were allowed to haul the tree to the car with the fragrance of balsam around us and the parents at our heels, debating the merits of this year's harvest.

As a city dweller, I find the process of getting a Christmas tree far easier and exciting in its own way, but hardly more rewarding. With no farms to speak of, we are forced to search other places for our trees. Like the hillsides of that farm in the country, the vacant lots of the city grow thick with groves of pine, fir, and spruce, starting soon after Thanksgiving. Families follow the same rituals of review, circling likely candidates, looking for the hidden qualities that make a tree special, imagining the way in which the blemishes of an otherwise perfect balsam might be hidden against a wall.

The other way to get a tree for your city home is to send for one through the mail. I tried this last year, on the grounds of professional curiosity and because something about raising a fir from Oregon in our Boston living room appealed to me. It arrived in a tiny carton, and I doubted it could ever again manage that nice pyramidal shape. But when I cut the twine binding the branches, they relaxed into their natural sweeping form. In a couple hours the luxurious scent of an Oregon forest spread through the house.

My father viewed my purchase as something between lunacy and indecency, but in the spirit of the season (and with the hope of rehabilitating me) he still allows us along on his annual treks. He now hunts for trees in a nearby national forest; all the same, the process is still a serious one, the results just as satisfying.

On cold mornings the birds huddle around our feeders like a construction crew around the canteen truck. The chickadees are the most numerous and most frequent visitors in this crowd, standing on the perches in their dusty-gray-and-white coats, their ruffed collars pulled up high and their black caps down snug on their heads. For simple pluck and sturdy good cheer I love the chickadee best. The trusting and outgoing manner of this frumpy little bird as well as its fierce loyalty (it will defend an area of up to twelve acres around its home) makes me feel I have a true companion in the creation and protection of my plot.

There is a charming everybird quality about chickadees. They are the birds I have known the longest. Throughout the winters in Vermont when I was growing up the chickadees were always a presence, sharing the single perch of a small feeder as my family ate breakfast on the other side of the kitchen bay window. It was one of my earliest chores to fill that red plastic feeder with sunflower seeds. It was a simple device that held little more than a cup; in the dead of winter the chickadees could empty the small feeder in a day. Our present feeder, which stands among a clump of deciduous holly, is more grand, but the birds are not put off by my pretensions, and I still relish this winter chore that calls me into the garden.

I share the birds' fondness for seeds, though they plant them with even less sense and greater abandon than I do. We both go into an uproar at the sight of a cat, and we take pleasure in singing in the garden, so long as we are alone. I favor a garden that is divided into rooms. I an pleased to discover chickadees also enjoy this style of design, though for different reasons. Breaking a garden into different regions allows them to set up house without worrying about invasions from other chickadees. I doubt my mixed borders and modest stretches of hedging satisfy their needs, but the idea pleases me. This sort of territorial aggressiveness is not uncommon to gardeners, either. I know numerous couples who have divided up their plots to avoid disputes.

My relations with chickadees and other birds are not always easy. I dislike their habit of coming around after I've sowed some new patch of lawn and devouring all the seeds, like teenage boys at a buffet table. And I wish they would leave the lettuce and radish seedlings alone as well. On the other hand, I don't care if they splurge on worms; I'll never eat one. I enjoy the collection of birds that gathers on our lawn every morning and their slow and stately stalking here and there, heads down with the intent look of someone deep in thought—or in search of a lost contact lens.

There is a bond between birds and gardeners that doesn't exist between gardeners and other animals, other gardeners included. It's easy enough to get by as a gardener without a groundhog or a family of mice. But a garden is a poor place without birds, whether a lone robin gathering supplies to build a nest or a congregation of sparrows holding a revival meeting among the branches of the mock orange. Like the grandfather clock whose chiming is so familiar you forget it, I count on the presence of the birds—their courting, their complaining, and most of all their quiet companionship.

Gardeners are almost perfectly suited to the holidays. In many respects they live in a year-long state of excitement and enchantment that most normal people know only in youth, and then only in December. Gardeners have a wide-eyed glee about all the seasons of the garden, be it the arrival of a shriveled and dormant tuber in October, the appearance of the nursery catalogs at the front door in December, the first spears of snowdrops in March, or the lavish unfurling of a new flower in June. The anticipation of a gardener waiting for a shipment matches that of the most holiday-crazed child, and surely most of them lie awake during the long winter nights to contemplate the treasures to come. I imagine some gardeners could even find a use for a lump of coal (as crocks in the bottom of a favorite pot, perhaps). In short, a gift of any sort—so long as it relates to the garden—is a delight.

But the pleasure of receiving a gift is matched equally by their desire to give, and a gardener is better than most other humans at giving gifts of that precious type—homemade. They will shower you with seeds, cut flowers, and cuttings. If you look twice at a plant, a gardener will immediately dig you a clump. The holiday spirit, or what we think of as the holiday spirit, courses through the blood of gardeners throughout the year.

At our house we like to pot up bulbs, which we then take around to neighbors sometime in the days before Christmas. Most often we have extra narcissus, but sometimes there are hyacinths and one year we had an excess of amaryllis. I collect clay pots from their storage area in their garage. It is important to let them warm up before washing them. If you dunk them in hot water too soon after bringing them in out of the cold, a number are sure to crack or break altogether. But the washing is essential, for I leave end-of-the-season cleaning to the start of the next season. Thus the pots are grimy with clods of soil and wisps of root clinging to their insides. This debris washes off easily enough and with it comes a musty odor that is refreshing at this time when many houses are choked with the scent of spiced cider and juniper.

This planting is our last chance of the year to scatter dirt around the kitchen, and we do so with all the energy of the other holiday activities. When we are done planting, we tie a bit of ribbon around each pot, tuck them all into cardboard boxes, and trundle them around to our neighbors. Except for the ribbon, these gifts aren't much to look at. But they offer promise—of color and fragrance to come in the new year.

FINIS.